DEVELOPING FAITH IN
Young Adults

EFFECTIVE

MINISTRY

WITH 18–35

YEAR OLDS

ROBERT T. GRIBBON

The Publications Program of The Alban Institute is assisted by a grant from Trinity Church, New York City.

Library of Congress Catalog Card Number 89-82320
ISBN #1-56699-036-X

CONTENTS

"Where are the young people who were raised in this parish? Why don't they come to church?" I heard those questions just today in a congregation that has had strong leadership and a stable population for many years. At the same time I note that a recent poll reports nearly 80 percent of college students say that religion is important in their lives. The tension between pastoral perspective and research data has been an ongoing reality in my ministry. In working with young adults, I have found an enduring contrast between low levels of participation and high levels of professed interest.

In the last quarter century, I have gone from being a coffee-house minister and campus chaplain to being one of those local church pastors who feels he is not doing enough about ministry with students and young adults. In between I spent many years researching and writing about young adult ministry. The purpose of this book is to consolidate the previous work, as well as to reflect on what has changed, what is enduring, and what learnings and tools are most useful from the perspective of a busy church pastor.

At least two historical changes affect the content of this research-based book. First, the "baby-boom" generation, as a major factor in young adult ministry has passed. The "Vietnam Generation" is no longer young. There are still a large number of people in the younger baby-boom cohort (born between 1955 and 1964) who may be entering church life in the early 1990s, but thereafter those in the young adult age bracket will be fewer, as already we have smaller numbers of eighteen-year-olds. Second, commuting and part-time college attendance are now the norm, although they were a new and unfamiliar phenomenon twenty-five years ago. Commuters are now the majority among college students. Although churches may still not have figured out how to minister to this segment of the young (and older) adult population, it seems unnecessary to explain at length the commuter experience and its impact on young adults.

The reader will find little here on the details of specialized young adult ministries such as campus ministry, military chaplaincy, or the urban singles' club. Settings with high concentrations of young adults have special needs. My concern here, however, is for the ordinary congregation that cannot provide specialized staff for young adult ministry and perhaps not even specialized programs. Are there some insights, theories, or tools which help one approach the young adult segment of the congregation? I ask myself, What is most helpful to me as a pastor now? What tools and theories have seemed most helpful to others as I have presented this material over the years? This book attempts to answer these questions.

This collection incorporates revisions of reflections and research previously published by The Alban Institute in *The Problem of Faith-Development in Young Adults, When People Seek the Church,* and *Half the Congregation.* In material I published in the past, I attempted to create workbooks that could take the place of workshops. A printed workbook, however, does not convey well or usefully the handouts and exercises that are so helpful in workshops. Thus I have chosen not to include in this book the history-gram, faith-development grid, or other exercises that work so well in group settings.

Looking at past published works, I note that the resource sections are the most out-of-date. Extensive footnoting has been omitted in favor of a bibliography of books referred to in the text and a section of notes that provide further information on nonpublished sources. The reader is encouraged to contact his or her denominational office for the latest resources. This is particularly important in regard to resources for addressing those issues which often form the content of young adult ministry programs: intimacy, sexuality, loneliness, relationships, career and lifestyle concerns, self-awareness, decision-making, financial management, survival skills, marriage, divorce, and parenting. These personal issues, together with spirituality and current social concerns, will probably always be a part of young adult ministry programming. They must be addressed in the most contemporary idiom, however, and from the particular perspective of each faith tradition or denomination. Thus the resources in these areas are very ephemeral.

Actually, all young adult ministry is ephemeral. Books and materials on ministry with young adults have been produced for at least seventy years, yet "young adult ministry" seems constantly being created as a new thing. Perhaps it is because young adults are forever young, the field is also. Because there is no abiding constituency for this ministry, its fortunes wax and wane in denominational offices as responsibilities are shifted. Reports and resources are circulated for a time in unpublished form, then pass out of date. People outgrow young adulthood, and few professionals devote a career to it. And so this book is dedicated with thanks to all those who have worked in the field of young adult ministry.

The many individuals from whom I have learned over the years and those who have furthered this work know who they are and don't need to be thanked here. However, appreciation should be expressed to those groups and agencies with whom I worked and who contributed to this work through their invitations to do projects and conduct workshops. They include the National Council of Churches Young Adult Ministry Team, the United States Army Chaplain Board, United Ministries in Higher Education, the American Baptist Church, the Episcopal Church, the Presbyterian Church, the United Church of Christ Board of Homeland Ministries, and several Annual Conferences of the United Methodist Church, among others. The Lilly Endowment funded the major part of the original research with twenty-nine congregations of various denominations. The Alban Institute housed this research for many years, and none of these manuscripts would have seen the light of day without the conscientious work of Celia Hahn and Grace Reggio.

We are particularly appreciative of all those who told their stories and experiences in interviews and workshops. Except where otherwise defined, the term "unchurched" is used as a shorthand way of referring to someone who does not participate in corporate worship apart from special occasions. Similarly, the term "dropout" refers to someone who at one time regularly participated in congregational activities and subsequently stopped or drastically reduced such activity. Both terms are used as a convenient shorthand but with some concern that they may be read pejoratively. No value judgement is intended in the use of these terms, and we acknowledge with thanks the contributions of several "dropouts" and "unchurched" persons to these studies. Further details of the various research projects referred to in the text are included in the notes at the back of the book.

Robert Gribbon

CHAPTER I

Young Adults and Developing Faith

The religious behavior of young adults is frequently baffling and frustrating. Despite years of effort put into Sunday schools and youth groups, most of the clergy look out over their congregations and see few young adults. Parents who have been faithful members for years don't know what to make of it when their children drop out of church or synagogue participation. Even professionals who minister with young adults find a strange dichotomy in their work; as one U.S. Army chaplain puts it, "The young soldiers that I work with all week and the Sunday congregation are two completely different groups." On the other hand, young adults often seem to be interested in college courses in religion, parachurch ministries, new age groups and bookstores, and other quasi-religious groups. Every metropolitan area seems to have a few churches about which the word is "they have hundreds of young people." Eighty percent of college students tell pollsters that religion is important in their lives.

After childhood the young clearly do not attend as frequently as their elders. That is a concern for church people, and it is often assumed to be a problem for which there must be a cause and a solution. Devout parents often first blame themselves when their children lose interest in church or synagogue and seem to stray from the fold. These parents believe that perhaps they didn't set a good enough example or they forced their children to attend too much or too little. Other parents may blame the institution: in the past, the Sunday school was too liberal or the rabbi didn't take an interest in youth; in the present, there are no activities for young adults, the church is too conservative, and so on.

Ministers may also blame themselves or the program for a lack of active young adults in the congregation. We find a widespread sense of failure and guilt about young adult ministry in churches and synagogues. Many people believe their congregation ought to have a young adult group or program, and they are frustrated by limited success.

Some other people place blame on the times or the culture. They say the times are changing and the young are rejecting the sterile conformity of traditional religion; others say society is becoming more secular, and the disaffection of the young from the church is one more sign of the crisis of the times. Others accuse the churches themselves of becoming too secular. An opposing and more phlegmatic view states that the young have always gone through a period of rebellion against parental and societal values. The young are expected to drop out of religious involvement but come back when they are settled. Overall, people commonly assume that the problem to be addressed is why young adults don't attend church. I want to address a larger question: How do we develop faith in young adults?

The question most frequently asked by church professionals and lay leaders is, How can we attract young adults? That question can be answered in part, but it has limitations as a basis for developing ministries with young adults. It assumes a commonality among young adults that is not supported in experience. No one approach will attract young adults, because so many differences exist among them. Their differences of cultural background, life situation, marital status, religious experience, and individual development are at least as great as, if not greater than, those of any other age group. Further, young adults related to church or synagogue are themselves a particular subgroup. Many programs built around the needs and interests of young adults affiliated with a congregation encounter the problem of not being able to interest nonaffiliated young adults, and programs designed for the nonaffiliated are often disappointing to congregational members. More than one church study has concluded that young adults are not a natural group for ministry.

A common assumption about young adult ministry is that its purpose is to get people "into the church." In some congregations, this concern is explicit and institutional: "Our congregation is getting smaller and older and we need young people in order to survive." Young adults of any age can add life to a congregation through their characteristic enthusiasm, willingness to try new things, emphasis on action, and fresh vision of the world. But many congregations won't welcome all these gifts. Although some congregations want new blood, they don't want new people. Old members may want new pledges to support the way things have always been. They may want new volunteers to support old activities, but not new activities. An older congregation that reaches out to young

adults will not find "people just like us." They will find a new generation, shaped by a different history. Although many of the new
people have similar basic values, they express them in new ways.
The older congregation will not be able to find replacements for
members who are dying, but will in some sense be creating a new
congregation. In order to reach out to these new people, the congregation must develop faith, confidence, trust within these new
people. Thus the question, How can we develop faith in young
adults? But before addressing this question, we need to identify
whom we are talking about. Who are young adults?

People use the term *young adult* in varied and sometimes con-
fusing ways. Informally, some people call younger teenagers young
adults, and some researchers and medical practitioners include
adults up to age forty in this category. Most denominations now define *young adults* as those eighteen to thirty-five years old. Taking
the broadest view of young adulthood we see that between ages
eighteen and forty people move from adolescence to mid-life.
These are the years of greatest physical energy and ability. These
are the years of entry into the work force, mating, childbearing, and
child rearing. Carl Jung sums up the first half of life as dominated
by the "outward journey" in which individuals focus energy on establishing relationships with others and the ego must create a place
for itself in the world of adults. Erik Erikson named the issues the
ego faces in these years *identity, intimacy,* and *generativity.* All
touch on young adulthood, and we might think of young adulthood
as a journey from identity concerns to generativity, but concerned
with issues of intimacy in different forms throughout the young
adult period. These themes of physical energy, directed outwards
towards establishment and intimacy, we see replayed in many forms
in young adult concerns with relationships, loneliness, career, failure, friendships, sex, and family. We turn now to look at young
adulthood more closely in three age groups which I refer to as *explorers, pioneers,* and *householders.*

Transitional young adults, generally between ages eighteen and
twenty-five, are the most mobile—in transition between school and
work and moving from life with parents to life on their own. These
explorers are open to experiments, to ideology, and to intense involvements. They are the least likely to attend church or synagogue
regularly. The special issues for faith development in this group are
addressed in Chapter II.

Adults in their midtwenties are establishing a "first adult life
structure" according to Daniel Levinson; we refer to them as *pioneers* because they are establishing a new world for themselves,
staking out their territory, doing many things for the first time. The

Alban 30+ research found this age-group the most likely to seek new congregational involvement and fertile ground for church growth and evangelism. This age-group is most likely to move into new communities. People who have dropped out of church during or after high school are most likely to return in this period. The Gallup poll conducted for the study "Faith Development in the Adult Life Cycle" found that

a. one-third of adults reported a significant faith change between ages sixteen and thirty;
b. for 80%, change in faith led to stronger faith;
c. the average age of significant faith change was twenty-eight.

Although Gail Sheehy calls the twenties the "decade of the 'should's,'" we found few young adults entering church life because they "should" attend. Their motivation is generally both more posi-tive and more tentative than that. These *novice* adults, both single and married, are looking for relationships with God and others: op-portunities to socialize and to work on issues related to intimacy. The process of affiliation with a congregation for this group is ad-dressed in Chapter III.

Adults in their late twenties or early thirties generally are more settled and have greater work, home, and community responsibilit-ies. They want to bring these concerns into congregational life. A majority are parents, and they like congregational activities for fami-lies. Education for children and child care during activities and meetings help their involvement. They need concrete opportunities for service and spiritual growth, support groups and ritual to help them with transitions and hard realities related to family conflict, ill-ness, death, and other loss. In the ancient Eastern description of the life cycle, those in this group are *householders,* and their spiritual growth is connected with their taking responsibility for the details of life. The issues related to this group are also addressed in Chap-ter III.

In its broadest definition, young adulthood ends with the begin-ning of the "mid-life transition," identified as a second major period for changes in faith in the study "Faith Development in the Adult Life Cycle." Chapter IV of this book further describes each of these groups of young adults with practical implications for congrega-tional ministry.

The three categories within the young adult period obviously overlap; characteristics and needs common to people at one age will often apply to individuals older or younger. Individual rates of development vary, society's expectations of age-appropriate behavior are becoming less rigid, and no age-related developmental schema of adult life is universally valid. These tags help us think about broad categories for ministry and are not intended as group labels. None of us likes to feel labeled and pigeonholed, and there is understandable resistance to labels like *senior citizen* or *young adult* that we put on age-groups. Such labels are not helpful to groups within the life of a congregation because they suggest that one group can meet the needs of everyone within an age span. It may make as much sense to have a young adult group as to have a middle-aged group.

In any case, age-specific programs are only a small part of ministry with young adults. Even when circumstances permit the formation of a group, a participation rate of 20 to 30 percent of the target population shows a good response. Congregations need to include younger adults in the community of faith and empower them for service in the world. In widely different congregations, we found young adults attracted by what they perceived as a living faith, convincingly believed and lived in relation to their world. We found that young adults who sought out the church were looking for a connection between transcendent reality and their day-to-day lives. In some places new congregations and parachurch organizations composed almost entirely of younger adults are springing up. However, for most of us the intergenerational congregation must be the norm, and it has certain advantages. Both young and old are enriched by the intergenerational mix.

As the pastor of a small congregation, I must deal with persons of all ages, including young adults. The numbers are not great enough for a young adult program, and I no longer have the automatic rapport that comes from being of the same generation. So I ask, What do I know that is useful to young adult ministry in this setting? One cannot assume that the statistics drawn from nationwide studies will be replicated in a sample as small as a single congregation, and certainly each individual whom we encounter is unique. However, I do find certain viewpoints useful in understanding young adults in my congregation, my community, and in the larger communities of faith and world. What follows is a summary of those perspectives.

The Historical Perspective

People are shaped by the history through which they have lived and in particular by those events occurring when they come of age. The one generic statement that we can make about all young adults is that they have lived through a history different from that of older members of the congregation. On the average, we can expect people to have some familiarity with major events that have occurred since they were eleven, but not before. This insight reminds me, as a preacher, that references to persons or events that were prominent more than six years ago are history to the youngest adults in my congregation. In workshops, we have found most effective those exercises that help people of different generations share the historical and cultural memories that have shaped their lives. Carrying this knowledge into pastoral work, I find it helpful to ask persons of all ages to share with me significant historical events they remember.

A further interpretation of the historical overlay helps me understand the perspectives of various groups within the congregation. Douglas Walrath in *Frameworks* (Pilgrim Press, 1987) has summarized the worldview and faith stance of three recent generations, which he labels *Strivers, Challengers,* and *Calculators.* The Strivers, born before 1931, were shaped by the Depression and World War II. They have experienced both adversity and change, but desire stability as the normal state of affairs—they tend to accept God and the institution of the church as essential and given. Challengers, shaped by the postwar years and the Vietnam experience, desire change and generally experience the church as one option among many, perhaps useful in the support of certain causes. The Calculators, born since 1954, have grown up in a world in which erosion and the experience of limits are normal. Compared to the older Challengers, Calculators are more careful in their choices, counting the costs. For them, piety and involvement in a congregation may provide resources to survive in a rapidly changing world.

We do not yet know how the next generation will experience the church and the world. We do know that those just coming into adulthood are most affected by the events of that time. The issues of one's coming-of-age tend to shape one's perspective throughout life. However, we are notoriously inept at understanding our own present moment or projecting future history. By way of example, the 1960s produced many predictions of "the greening of America" by the emerging "consciousness III" and "postmaterialism"—predictions now best left buried. Similarly, we may read "this generation will not be seduced by the glories of militarism"—a statement written in a young adult manual of 1938 about those whose shaping experience became World War II.

If some writers place their extravagant hopes for the future on today's young people, who will somehow be brighter, wiser, and kinder, others see a countertrend. Since before the time of Socrates, there has been a tendency to see the emerging generation as uncouth, lacking in faith and morals, disrespectful of tradition. A fourteenth-century critic complains that the young people only come to church at Christmas and Easter, and then only to look at the hats and low-cut dresses. From any theological perspective, the young obviously are neither better nor worse than anyone else. But we need to withdraw both our fears and our fantasies about them if we are to treat them as persons and develop faith in them.

The generation coming of age will reflect the tendencies of the time, but in a more pronounced form because there is no countervailing experience. Two examples illustrate the point. First, at any time the chief concern of the American adult population as reported in survey polls will also be the salient public concern of those from age eighteen to twenty-two. Second, this latter age-group attended church in greater numbers than the general population in only one recorded year, 1957, which was also the peak of church attendance for the U.S. population. Whatever the tendency of the times, young adults will reflect it in a pronounced form. The young mirror and magnify where we are *now*.

Finally, this discussion merits a note on what was once called the generation gap. Despite the ongoing apparent clash of cultures, the evidence is that there has never been a generation gap, only differences between classes and subcultures within the society. Eighty percent of the time, by age twenty-five people end up with 80 percent of the operative values of their parents. The balance of the generational strife is a temporary developmental phenomenon as young adults struggle with identity, independence, and sexuality. Since we first had opinion polls, the young have always appeared more liberal on lifestyle issues, or, as Alistair Cooke intones, "Each generation of this century has been convinced that it was the one which made the break with Victorian morality."

The Developmental Perspective

"A chaos of the mind and body—a time for weeping at sunsets and at the glamour of moonlight—a confusion and profusion of beliefs and hopes, in God, in Truth, in Love, and in Eternity—an ability to be transported by the beauty of physical objects—a heart to ache or swell—a joy so joyful and a sorrow so sorrowful that oceans could lie between them: then, as a counterpoise to these attractive features, outcrops of selfishness indecently exposed—restlessness or inability to settle down and stop bothering the middle-aged—pert argument on abstract subjects like Beauty, as if they were of any interest to the middle-aged—lack of experience as to when truth should be suppressed in deference to the middle-aged—general effervescence and nuisance and unfittingness to the set patterns of the seventh sense—these must have been some of Guenever's characteristics at twenty-two, because they are everybody's." Whether we agree with all the details from T. H. White's description in *The Once and Future King*, our recognizing what he is talking about demonstrates the point that certain traits are characteristic of young adulthood.

All the works on young adult ministry written in this century have attempted to trace the psychological profile of young adults, and in the past fifteen years we have seen a lot of popular attention given to the passages and stages of adult life. However, the more detailed this literature becomes, the less helpful I find it for ordinary parish ministry. As a pastor, I am constantly dealing with individual lives that are not predictable from the general statistics, and my job is more to respond to where people are than to predict where they might be.

Yet a general knowledge of the life cycle and the broad process of development is helpful in listening to people. I find these theories help me enter their perspective more easily and help orient me to the flow of their lives. Thus the theories of Erik Erikson, Jane Lovinger, Daniel Levinson, Carol Gilligan, Robert Kegan, and others can all be useful as a kind of basic orientation, in the same way that knowledge of the work of Elisabeth Kubler-Ross can help one understand the grief without imposing a rigid framework on the hapless bereaved.

The model of development from adolescence to adulthood (presented more fully in Chapter II) can be used as an orienting perspective, but with the following proviso. A number of factors are changing the process of coming-of-age and the images of adulthood in America. On the one hand, young people are required to make major life-style decisions at younger ages; on the other, our image of adulthood is not one of being settled for life. Rather, adults are expected to continually adjust their lives to changing circumstances, and the process of coming-of-age is one of learning to make appropriate decisions rather than simply coming to the point of having decided once regarding career, mate, and life-style. Although younger and older adults will continue to have different concerns and characteristic styles, the changed nature of adulthood makes our equality as fellow pilgrims more obvious.

This last point warrants one more illustration. Fifteen years ago, Bob Ross could write about a new stage of life, the young adult period of *transadulthood,* a longer transitional period between adolescence and adulthood in which young adults were less likely to settle down and more concerned to keep their options open. Today we see many adults of all ages opting for that lifestyle, while other young adults make early commitments to a particular track. In fact, it is more difficult today for young adults to find a transitional space, a place or period of time in which they may experience what Erikson called a *moratorium,* an opportunity to experiment with belief and behavior without major consequences.

Finally, the developmental perspective reminds us of the obvious—people are not the same at age twenty as at forty or sixty or eighty. Twenty has more energy, fewer memories, an orientation to the present and the future. Commitment styles and major preoccupations are different. The developmental viewpoint gives a quick way to keep in mind the needs of younger as well as older adults in our presentations and planning.

The Faith Development Perspective

A part of the attention to developmental stages in recent years has been the work of James Fowler and others in the area of faith development. In 1985 a major project sponsored by the Religious Education Association and others conducted both a nationwide telephone poll of over 1,000 people and 41 interviews in depth to test various hypotheses related to faith development. Neither sample supported a correlation between age and faith stage or faith change in adulthood. However, the data do support the idea that young adulthood, like other periods of life, is a period of faith change, and two-thirds of Americans now expect that faith should change, over the life cycle. Insofar as any correlation exists between faith stage and life stage, it has more to do with life-changing events experienced than with chronological age. These data reinforce our belief that while the cultural language and life issues of younger adults may differ from their elders, the underlying religious quest and questions are very similar. (For a summary of the project learnings, see *Faith is a Verb* by Kenneth Stokes, Twenty-Third Publications, 1989.)

In some areas of *saliency,* adults under thirty show a pattern statistically different from their elders. Younger adults are less likely to report that religion is "very important" in their lives, or that they have "a great deal of faith currently," or that they attended church or synagogue in the past seven days. However, even the most extreme differences reported between those under thirty and those over fifty amount to twenty percentage points at most. For example, about one-third of adults under thirty attend church in any given week while nearly one-half of those over fifty do. Even this much statistical difference may not be relevant when we are dealing with an individual or a small group. However, perhaps enough difference exists to support the broad generalization that young adults exhibit the phenomenon of "belief without belonging," characterized by high levels of belief and lower levels of involvement or confidence in local church institutions.

Overall similarities in the statistical pattern obscure some similarities and differences among selected populations. For example, over the past thirty years, the participation rates by age for Roman Catholics have swung widely, being influenced first by the Vatican II reforms and then by an influx of young Hispanics. In contrast, among Protestants, the attendance rate difference between those under and over age thirty has been a pretty constant 10 percent over the past twenty years. Even within this difference there continues to be an age-specific effect as the transitional young adults from age eighteen to twenty-two tend to reduce their church affiliation, and in their middle to late twenties affiliate with another religious group in a new community. Although the overall numbers change little, the individual may experience a great deal of faith change or reassessment in young adulthood. In particular, the traditional college years (age eighteen to twenty-two) continue to be a special period of development in faith, and the nuances of mentoring in this period are well developed in Sharon Parks' *The Critical Years* (Harper and Row, 1986). We find the early fourfold faith development schema proposed by John Westerhoff (experience, affiliation, search, ownership), while not accurate in some ways, continues to be a framework that young and older adults can quickly grasp and use to describe their own faith story, particularly during the young adult years. (See Chapter II for a discussion of Westerhoff's schema).

In all of this work, we are well aware that the spiritual journey, one's personal walk with God, is not the same as church participation. Indeed, we talked to more than one person whose faith sustained their absence from the church. But even major experimentation with alternative religions has not changed the overall pattern of dropping out and reaffiliation. Statistical studies of the U.S. population have borne out our predictions that the baby-boom generation would return to church participation despite massive defections in the sixties and seventies. The statistical analysis of the return rate was done by David Roosen of Hartford Seminary and continues to be evidenced in the high participation rates reported in the Gallup poll mentioned earlier.

The Demographic Perspective

At this point, the local church leader may feel some exasperation and ask, If young adult participation rates continue to be only a few points lower than the national average, where are all those people? Why don't I see them in my church? The populations of young adults and, in particular, of church-going young adults are not evenly distributed. Never-married young people are among those least likely to attend church, and these young singles tend to congregate in certain neighborhoods—there the church must develop a specialized ministry with singles. Although it is untrue that young married people only attend church "for the sake of the kids," in America historically there has been a correlation between family values, the rate of family formation, and church attendance. Today that correlation is seen geographically when the young adult attenders are most likely to be seen clustered in congregations in the starter suburbs and the "blue-collar nurseries." The churches of the old mainline Protestant denominations are less likely to see these people for two reasons. First, the appeal of these churches is directed more to the upper middle class, which has a lower birthrate, deferred childbearing, and less commitment to those family values. Second, the actual church buildings of these denominations are more likely to be located in established neighborhoods in which neither young families nor young singles can afford housing.

American neighborhoods and congregations are highly segregated by level of income and therefore by class and age. Churches that are booming are those that are located where the people are and have adapted themselves to the lifestyle of the surrounding culture. We know that in religion, as in other areas of life, an old style of brand loyalty no longer holds. Instead, the young (and others) are responding to that local convenient church which responds to their needs for meaning and belonging in warm and friendly ways, spoken in their language and style.

Within the age span from eighteen to thirty-five great differences are obvious in socioeconomic status, racial background, political attitude, religious belief, and personal situation; such differences may be more important than any commonality of age. Not every congregation needs specialized ministries to all ages. However, a congregation's neighborhood may call that congregation to pay attention to ministry with a particular age group when the population tends to be age-segregated because of patterns of housing and employment. For example, a congregation in a college town may have many transitional adults. A church located in a "condo canyon" of

high-rise condominiums and efficiency apartments may have a particular ministry with young single adults. A congregation sur-
rounded by small single-family houses may discover that its neighborhood has become a starter suburb where families with young
children seek homes. Within the past fifteen years, the PRIZM system and similar cluster-based marketing systems have developed
the ability to pinpoint the age and class profile of every zip code
and census tract in America. (See *The Clustering of America* by Michael J. Weiss, Harper and Row, 1988.) Data from such marketing
systems document the intuitive observation that young adults are
found in some areas, not others, and that great differences exist in
the lifestyle of young adults from one neighborhood to another. Increasingly, the American market is becoming fragmented and specialized, and this is true for programs and publications as well as
goods and services, which may mean that any generalizations about
what young adults are like become increasingly less useful.

The People Perspective

In general, we have noted that the term *young adult* does not des-
ignate a focus for ministry because it is so broad; however, within
any particular community, enough similarity among the young
adults may exist to use age as a focus for ministry. For places where
that is true, and the congregation is large enough, Terry Hershey
has produced an excellent step-by-step guide for developing a program. (See *Young Adult Ministry* from Group Books, Loveland, Col-
orado, 1986) Another approach is to focus not on age but on ministry with single persons, who now make up over one-third of the
adult population in the United States. This can be an intergenerational approach that will include many young adults. Many resources are available for singles ministry, which is a specialty of its
own. However, it is well to remember that even the best program
will not involve more than one-third of the identified target group
within the congregation.

Perhaps the ideal situation for young adult ministry is to live in
one of those neighborhoods where young adults form a high percentage of the population. There they can be brought into the faith
community to shape it with their unique culture, perspectives, gifts,
and energy. But, in most congregations young adults will be a minority and lack status—they haven't been around so long, and they
don't contribute as much as the pillars of the church. There is a
real as well as a perceived power differential between the young
and older adults in the church. However progressive we may think

we are, those of us in positions of leadership tend to represent the centuries of tradition, the investment in buildings, the interests of the existing institution—and we have the power to back that up. Without our being aware of it, younger adults may feel shut out.

But the young need to participate. The church needs their input, and they need to find a place in the adult structure as a part of finding a place in the world and the community of believers as an adult. A number of factors naturally work against the full and influential participation of younger adults, and, therefore, this is an area most congregations need to approach intentionally. Again, it is older people who need to reach out to include, because they believe in young adults.

Programs don't work, people do. In all the various settings for young adult ministry that we have studied—campuses, congregations, military bases—it is apparent that even those programs that can be transferred from one place to another soar in one setting and bomb in another. The key ingredient in effective young adult ministries appears to be people—specifically, energetic, faithful leaders respectful of young adults. This point may seem obvious and applicable to any form of ministry, but it is especially relevant to young adult ministry.

As young people enter the adult world, test the dreams of childhood, experiment, and form, as Levinson describes it, a "first adult life structure," there is an underlying search and hope for life as authentic, joyful, worth it—that it is untrue that "life goes on, long after the thrill of living is gone." If the congregation's representatives seem burned-out, dead, inauthentic, or out-of-touch, they will not commend themselves. As William G. Perry commented about students moving into the advanced stages of commitment and finding an adult teacher who seemed to be living with some conviction, "They will beat on you to see if you are for real." (*Forms of Intellectual and Ethical Development in the College Years,* Holt, Rinehart & Winston, 1968) Young adults still need what Erikson called guarantors, people who in some sense guarantee the possibility of the adult life toward which the young strive. At the same time, that adult guarantor must believe in the young adult at a time when the young person may be assailed by doubt or be maintaining a shallow self-sufficiency, what Gail Sheehy calls "the tyranny of the should's." The attitude required of an older adult comes down to a respect for the individual, or in a larger sense, a faith in young adults.

Respect for young adults implies a valuing of who they are now, as well as who they may become. This past summer my church lost one of our sixteen-year-old camp counselors in an automobile accident. We were reminded again that this life was full, complete, valued by God—just like the life of one buried at age ninety-two. The contribution of this young person was greater than that of many persons four times his age. Death reminds us of the present value of each life. Young adults themselves seldom think of their own death, but for them also the present is most important—not who they were or what they may someday be. Those who work with young adults need a full respect for that present reality of the individual. As I work now in the parish with many different ages, from young children to the elderly, I find that I don't have a theory about young adult ministry—with every age "I just treat 'em like people." But the theories help me hear the individuals rather than impose my own reality.

The perspectives discussed above can help achieve respect for young adults as persons. First, we recognize that the young adult before us comes out of a historical experience different from our own. Without judging that experience, we accord it the same respect we would that of someone from a different culture or language group. Then we recognize the gifts and dilemmas of his or her point in life as God-given. God creates and sustains the developmental process. Knowing this, we recognize the faith journey of the person before us as having its own validity. The faith the person before us brings is complete, the sum of a life to this point, and to that extent equivalent to our own. Yet, we may recognize that the predominant style through which faith is expressed is different from our own because there have been different life experiences. What I am suggesting in regard to faith might be understood through an analogy with the experience of love. We can rejoice with young persons in their experience of falling newly in love, even though our own current experience may be the deep joy of a twenty-year marriage. Finally, we welcome and invite into full participation all whom God sends to us, remembering that many have already been made full members of the community of Faith.

We recognize and respect the developmental and cultural differences of those we deal with. The developmental perspective helps us understand where this person is coming from, what the major life issues are. On the cultural side, we can respect the need for every age and every culture, even every neighborhood, to work out their own salvation in fear and trembling. I recall Jim Adams (rector of St. Mark's Church on Capitol Hill in Washington, D.C.) saying in reflection on his move as a young clergyman from a blue-collar suburb to Capitol Hill, "I had been fighting with those people about a lot of things that had nothing to do with the Gospel." In the missionary work of the church, we have learned, by and large in the twentieth century, to avoid cultural imperialism as we attempt to take the faith to people of every tribe and nation in their own language, to be expressed in their own rhythms and mores. Now that the rate of social change is so great that every generation represents a new culture, we must find ways to share our faith that overcome our own cultural and historical bias. To those who want to develop the faith of young adults, we would say what we say to any missionary: first, love the Lord your God, and second, love those to whom you are sent. Thus we say, love God, and love young adults.

CHAPTER II

The Path of Faith Development in Young Adults

The Early Adult Transition

The period between ages seventeen and twenty-four may be the most critical period for the development of faith after age two. These are the years of formation or indoctrination in military training, monastic orders, cults, and academic or professional disciplines. But these are also the years people are least likely to be in church or synagogue. The picture has not changed much since twenty years ago the massive study of Lutherans age fifteen to sixty-five found that those nineteen to twenty-three years old were the least likely to be involved in congregational life and the most likely to be engaged in "Questionable personal activities." *(A Study of Generations)*. At the same time, the study found this group demonstrated the greatest openness to change, and showed the *lowest* need for unchanging structure, the least generalized prejudice, the least acceptance of middle-class norms, and the least desire for distance from differing social and religious groups. (Strommen 1972) In every survey of the U.S. population since 1957, when young adults are compared with other groups, the young adults are less likely to be churchgoers, and they report a lower rate of involvement in religious activities other than services of worship. On broad statistical measures, young adults eighteen to twenty-four years old are about ten percentage points less likely than the average American to be a church member, to attend church, or to view religion as important. This has been true in the U.S. for a number of years. (As we will see later, for the most part, the decline in congregational participation among young adults is a developmental phenomenon related to their age, rather than a long-term disaffiliation.

Basic Transitions in Young Adulthood

What does society expect? What is required to be an adult? In the recent past, the passage of young adulthood could be understood through the stereotype of a young man who left home around age eighteen and by age thirty had settled down with a wife, two children, mortgage, membership in the PTA, local service club, and church. The intervening years might be marked by college, military service, and transitional jobs, but there was a fair degree of personal independence and mobility.

In the United States today, the eighteen-year-old is an adult, past high school graduation and the strict age segregation of the public school system, and is able to vote and serve in the armed forces. However, society often does not expect a full measure of adulthood from the young adult. We expect some transition between the dependence of childhood and the full interdependence of adulthood. The eighteen-year-old attending college who lives with a parent continues some of the dependencies of childhood. On the other hand, a twenty-five-year-old may experience increasing success at work, have children to care for, and be looking for a house while evidencing a greater concern about the neighborhood. The transition between these states has been described as a move from dependence to interdependence with a transitional period of freedom from responsibility in between.

A major step in achieving independence from parents and a place in the larger society is getting a regular paying job. The ability to "do a day's work for a day's pay" is an indicator of adult status. Generally, young people must become self-supporting and contributing members before they are accorded full adult status in a society. For most young people in industrialized countries today, the years prior to age eighteen are years of preparation. The young adult period begins with testing various vocational possibilities through apprenticeships, entry-level jobs, or educational programs. Usually there follow one or two trials of vocational options or transitional jobs before a vocational direction is set. The poor generally have fewer options and are required to make a living earlier in life, while others cannot find any job that would affirm their adult status and value in society.

In traditional societies, some rite of passage marked the transition to adulthood at ages much earlier than eighteen. The rite of passage was often preceded by teaching in the lore of the tribe and by tests of adulthood, but it occurred chronologically about when an individual could take on adult tasks. Jesus, in traditional Jewish society, would have learned the basics of his trade by age thirteen. Not too long ago, a boy from a farm family might be able to do "a man's work." In our complex technical society, a young man or woman may not finish professional preparation until the late twenties because affluence makes it possible to prolong dependence; the many roles open in a complex society make choices more difficult; and advanced technical jobs require an extended period of preparation.

Although the trains may no longer run, there are still college towns centered on the railroad depot in parts of the United States. Similarly, our notions of young adult ministry and faith development may be fixed on the patterns of a former time. It may not stretch the point too much to say that railroads, higher education, and adolescence developed together in this country. Although great universities existed for centuries, the expansion of higher education was fueled by industrialization, the expansion of the upper middle class, and the need for more scientifically educated workers. (Who before the nineteenth century would have thought of an agricultural college?) In a rural society with limited mobility, most young people grew up and lived in one community, learning a trade from parents or other adults in the community. If they went to church, families went together. Industrialization separated home and workplace, and after the abolition of child labor, created the need for extended schooling, first in high schools. The years of schooling continued dependence past the point of biological and sexual maturity, contributing greatly to what was once widely discussed as the "storm and stress" of adolescence.

By the beginning of the twentieth century, 9 percent of eighteen-year-olds were going to college, and they went *away* to college, often arriving at the local railroad depot with trunks for the school term. In general, the ideal college on the American scene was a residential institution, built "fifty miles from the nearest known sin." Up through the 1950s such colleges and even the large state universities functioned *in loco parentis* for students, prescribing detailed rules of personal conduct and providing a wide variety of activities. Because such schools were total environments in which students lived and worked, it was natural that churches would provide ministries and centers for those students. Throughout the first two-thirds of the twentieth century, the percentage of American youth completing high school and the percentage going on to college increased.

The forms of ministry handed down to us developed out of a sincere desire to be in ministry with young people in particular settings, and those forms were shaped by certain environments. The urban YMCAs and YWCAs were first created to provide healthy residential settings for young people coming to the cities to work. Likewise, the scouting movement, youth groups, and later young couples clubs were created at times when they fulfilled specific needs. Religious student centers at colleges were created when students were resident on campus for long periods and needed a place to gather. Certainly not everyone went to college or even finished high school. But the experience of large numbers who did continues to shape our understandings of development, shapes even the available research, and certainly shapes our forms of ministry.

Around the turn of the century, the literature on adolescence also expanded, much of it from denominational presses as religious leaders tried to figure out how to teach and lead those in this new world between childhood and adulthood. By 1920 Fredrick Tracy, a student of G. Stanley Hall, could write, "That period of life technically known as Adolescence, untechnically as the time of Youth, and colloquially as the Teen Age, covering the years from the advent of puberty to the attainment of maturity, and roughly identical with the days of high school and college education, has been widely and carefully studied, from every point of view in recent years. . . ." (The Psychology of Adolescence) The traditional college years from age eighteen to twenty-two were sometimes considered late adolescence, sometimes young adulthood, but always as a transitional phenomenon. At one point it was expected that children would leave the parental home, go off to college (a place of controlled folly as well as disciplined study), and graduate in four years prepared to begin a career as men and women ready to settle down in the world. Others less affluent or gifted would need to make their transitions in other ways, through apprentice trades, military service, or early marriage.

Either in college or perhaps in the military, it was expected that one would become ready to be an adult. Robert J. Havinghurst, working in the 1940s and early 1950s, was one of the pioneers in the application of the *developmental task* concept. In the late adolescent period, he includes the tasks of "developing personal independence" and "developing a philosophy of life." The eight tasks of his period *early adulthood* were "selecting a mate, learning to live with a marriage partner, starting a family, rearing children, managing a home, getting started in an occupation, taking on civic responsibility, and finding a congenial social group." (*Human Development and Education,* 1953) Clearly the image of late adolescence and early adulthood is one of transition before settling down.

Havinghurst goes on to identify other tasks later in adulthood, but only in the last twenty years have we seen the plethora of books on adulthood itself as a time of change, crisis, and development. In fact, the common experience of many people now is one of career, family, and geographic change throughout adulthood—thus children experience these changes too. Insofar as it is possible to speak now of an *early adult transition* (Levinson's term) in the period from seventeen to twenty-five years of age, it is a transition not from childhood to adulthood but from legal dependence to a first adult life structure (See Chapter I). The early adult transition is not *the* transitional period but one among many.

Of course no summary can do justice to the reality. Even full volumes on young adult development must generalize and cannot adequately convey the rich complexity of individual journeys, for example, the seventeen-year-old mother, the twenty-year-old AIDS victim, or the twenty-two-year-old officer in the missile silo—all of whom must face life, death, and responsibility beyond what we associate with the transitional years. The theories and general descriptions of development help us organize what we observe, but cannot teach us what we have not observed. Further, it must be acknowledged that any such descriptions are to some extent class-bound, culture-bound, gender-bound. Erik Erikson's work is still the most grounded in cross-cultural observation, but some consider his language and concepts gender-biased. But Erikson himself always reminds us that development is psychosocial, the intersection of internal and universal issues with challenges, opportunities, and roles provided by a particular culture.

One relevant example of the interaction of inner and outer forces comes to us from a study of French-speaking Roman Catholic college students in Quebec. (*Identity and Faith in Young Adults*, Lorimer, et. al., Paulist Press, 1973) The researchers noted a decrease in church participation, but did not find it to result from pervasive doubt or a crisis of faith. Rather they found four factors operating at the same time: (1) The internal development of critical thinking (Jean Piaget's *formal operations*) coincided with exposure to the relativistic mind-set of the university, weakening the absolute truth-claims of faith; (2) internal "lustful strivings" led to sexual experimentation at odds with church teaching, so students avoided church to avoid guilt feelings; (3) moving away from home decreased the affective ties that involved them in a home church community, and this energy was often invested in nonchurch friends or causes at the university; and (4) decreasing religious practice was an easy form of rejecting parental authority and childhood values in the struggle for autonomy. Obviously many of these same factors continue to operate today with our students and young adults, and we can still document age eighteen as the median and modal point for dropping out of church-participation. However, that is not to claim that dropping out at age eighteen is a universal, necessary, desirable, or biologically determined phenomenon.

Similarly, a conjunction of inner and outer forces initiates young adulthood at age eighteen in the U.S. Eighteen is the legal age of emancipation, and for the majority age seventeen marks graduation from the age-segregated structure of high school. Biology and culture point one towards adulthood. The young adult may be headed for further education, but knows that one must establish one's own place in society. That means finding a job. It means testing one's own abilities, interests, and self-concept against what is valued in the larger society. In our culture, adulthood means a kind of autonomy, giving up psychological and economic dependence on one's parents. It means finding out what one believes for oneself. It means finding a consistent identity with peers and exploring possibilities of intimacy. It means accepting responsibility for one's decisions and commitments.

Young adults in this early adult transition are generally very mobile. The U.S. Census Bureau reports that adults in the age range from twenty-two to twenty-four change address more frequently than any others. These young adults generally share a psychological as well as a physical mobility. They can respond quickly to a spur-of-the-moment invitation, they are free to "go with the flow," and are often able to form intense relationships quickly. They may become intensely involved in a project, cause, or major interest, and within a matter of months move on to something else. (In contrast, older adults are apt to become involved more slowly and make commitments on a more limited, but long-term, basis.)

Especially in the early years of the transition, young adults may use a variety of tactics—at one moment counterdependent, rejecting authority, the next identifying with the positions and postures of a respected teacher. Various roles and behaviors may be tried on and experimented with. A group of friends may provide a transitional substitute family while parental ties are broken. The young adult may become intensely committed to an ideological position, or may seem to hold all convictions at arms length, suspending belief in a kind of moratorium.

Individuals frequently enter young adulthood full of great hopes and confidence. They can exasperate their elders by their seeming inability to understand the limitations, failures, problems, and complexities of life. But for some young adults, limited affirmation from the world, rejection by others, failure of self-concept, or inability to make the world personally meaningful can result in disaster. The leading causes of death among transitional young adults stem from accidents and suicide.

Traditionally, societies have made room for experimentation and failure in the transition to adulthood. Provision has been made for experimentation and transitional identities. Our residential colleges were places where, with some protection from immediate consequence, one could learn, experiment, and test one's powers with the support of adult mentors and a community of peers.

Those peers and mentors are still needed, but the institutions that once held the transition are changing, the transition is no longer from one static role to another (if adulthood was ever static), and the duration of the transition has increased. In fact, in *The Critical Years,* Sharon Parks makes a good case for young adulthood as a period with a distinct integrity and stability of its own within adulthood, not simply a transitional period. We will return to her insights later, but first we will look more explicitly at faith development as it has been understood.

Faith Development

Must every individual be converted, or is it possible to be so nurtured in the faith that one grows up never knowing oneself not a Christian? Is adolescence and young adulthood the natural period of conversion or the natural time of apostasy? After analyzing many religious journals from the past as well as making contemporary observations of students, John Westerhoff, in *Will Our Children Have Faith,* proposes a description of how various styles of faith emerge in a person brought up within a faith community.

He speaks of faith growing in four concentric circles like the rings of a tree. He calls the four styles *experienced* faith, *affiliative* faith, *searching* faith, and *owned* faith. The styles as described by him are not age related, but may *tend* to be sequentially dominant at certain periods for a person who grows up in a faith community.

If we think of these styles for a moment as stages, we can say that *experienced faith* develops earliest. In the first six years of life the child learns through touch and experience to trust parental figures, the world, and God. The religious experience of children is often very fresh and personal.

Affiliative faith develops most easily in the school years, when we learn the story and rules of our community. We learn who our people are, we learn to belong. At school we say the Pledge of Allegience, at church we learn Bible stories. We derive a sense of who we are from affiliation with the community.

In the later teenage years, as independence and personal identity develop, there follows a period of *searching faith,* marked by questioning, experimentation, acting over against the community, and commitment to various ideologies and causes.

On this basis of experience, affiliation, and personal searching, an *owned faith* may develop in the form of a more personal, integrated stance that is not based solely on the received beliefs of the community. Owned faith is marked by a willingness to make commitments, and may lead to new commitment to the church.

But *real* faith is not a matter of age or style. Each of the four styles can express sincere, deep, and authentic faith. We all continue to need to experience the reality of God, to affiliate with others on the basis of shared beliefs; we continue to search and question as well as make commitments on the basis of what we most deeply believe. In Alban studies we have used Westerhoff's schema with many people to talk about their own journeys, and most people find it helpful and true for them, while many note that the cycle of the four stages can take place at any point in life. Young adults often find the schema helpful in making sense of their own searching.

In general, the faith of young adults is marked by questioning of values and religion, experimentation, and exploratory commitments. The value of Westerhoff's perspective is in seeing these activities as a positive form of faith, one that is necessary for a more inclusive and personal adult commitment. But there are many roads that people take.

A minority of young adults are attracted to groups that seem to offer certainty and support, a sense of place and belonging over against the loneliness described as a problem by many young adults. Other young adults simply maintain an affiliative style, perhaps retaining outward forms while struggling intellectually. The most common pattern for church-related youth is to drop out of active church involvement in the teenage years. Adult practice seems boring; childhood belief seems outgrown, but there is not yet a commitment to take its place. As a young adult, the individual may engage in an active searching that leads to commitment. Or if the search is too frightening or unproductive, he or she may withdraw from the search, finding a limited comfort and significance in friends, family, and career. Indeed, most of the people we see returning to church involvement in the middle to late twenties come not with a sense of conviction but with a tentative, exploratory, or wistful attitude. Several pastors have noted the need for young adults to recapitulate Westerhoff's four stages at that point of reentry (or first affiliation when that is the case).

Most that we have said so far applies to almost all young adults. In describing identity, intimacy, and generativity, Erik Erikson is speaking of issues that face all human beings as they age. In North American society, almost all are expected to achieve economic independence from parents, and a degree of personal autonomy is expected by the midtwenties. The sorting through childhood beliefs is common. But in some young adults, particularly on college campuses, we may see a sustained intellectual searching and a further kind of stage development.

Back in the 1950s, William G. Perry was involved in helping Harvard students learn to study, and he observed an interesting phenomenon: otherwise bright students frequently couldn't understand exam questions when asked to compare and contrast different viewpoints. Especially as entering freshmen, they were confused, and wanted to know what the right answer was. After years of careful interviews with Harvard and Radcliffe students, Perry went on to describe a process of development in which over a period of years individual students moved away from an attitude that there were simple, right or wrong answers dependent on external authority. The students moved through a stage of *multiplicity,* thinking that there were many answers, to a stage of *relativism,* in which there seemed no sure ground of intellectual or personal decision making. Beyond that crisis, students became increasingly able to take responsibility for a personal stance, making commitments that would undergird intellectual pursuit and moral action. *(Intellectual and Ethical Development in the College Years)*

Other researchers have described parallel developments often taking place at this stage of life. For example, Lawrence Kohlberg describes the development of moral reasoning from a "good boy-nice girl orientation through a law and order stage, followed sometimes by "hedonistic regression" before a principled, "postconventional," "social contract" orientation. Jane Loevinger describes the development of the ego from conformist to self-aware to conscientious stages.

Many other researchers have explored this territory, notably, James Fowler, to whom Westerhoff acknowledges a debt. Fowler has carefully described six stages of faith, two of which parallel this movement from an external to an internal locus of authority. At the third of Fowler's stages, the individual more or less uncritically accepts the conventions of his or her primary reference groups. The individual may not always conform to the expectations and may be opposed to certain teachings or authorities, but criticism is within the basic assumptions of the system. For example, the frequent charge that churches are hypocritical assumes a tacit acceptance of their standards. Likewise, the person may express conflict with authorities in terms of other authorities, for example, saying, "He's not a good minister—he doesn't teach the Bible right." The conventions held by a group are not necessarily shared in the wider society. Illustrating this point is a quip, intended as a put-down, made about youth in the sixties: "In rebellion against conformity they all dressed in exactly the same way."

Fowler's third or *conventional* stage is also described as *synthetic* because the individual relates not just to one but to several reference groups and tacitly adopts differing conventions. For example, a student may move between classroom, fraternity house, hometown, and business world, adapting to each without really noticing differences in their worldviews. Aware of using different values in different settings, the student is not particularly troubled.

But in Fowler's fourth stage, the individual has become aware of a tension between conflicting claims, and attempts to establish a point of view outside the communities of reference. In the process, the individual becomes more self-aware. The personal point of view tends to be articulated, explicit, and defined at this stage, rather than tacit. According to Fowler, symbols are more apt to be explained and reduced to stated meanings at this stage than at any other. A question like, Tell me what your faith means to you? is more readily answered at this stage than at others.

Fowler notes that many young adults seem to be in a three-to-four transition, and Sharon Parks has expanded this developmental period into a stage in its own right. Parks urges us not to see any part of young adulthood as merely transitional, but as a unique stage of human life, one in which the dream or vision or ideal that undergirds all of life is formed. In Parks' description, the young adult has moved away from what has been inherited, but is not yet restrained by adult commitments. Authorities are no longer given, but are self-chosen, as are the young adult's mentors and communities. Such communities are frequently ideologically grounded, as evaluations of self and society composed in terms of an ideal. Because of this, and because the individual's inner dependence is still fragile, Parks notes a special vulnerability about young adult life.

Again, the young adults with whom Parks is most familiar are university students. In larger samples of adults, both Fowler and Loevinger find a majority of adults in the midranges of their scales. Most adults fit neither the standards of those who see religious belief in terms of unswerving loyalty to one external authority, nor the expectations of those who see articulate, individualized commitment as the mark of true faith. Those who work with young adults can expect to find individuals who are at various points of faith development.

Ministry and Faith Development Theory

College chaplains have long noted that apart from that majority who were seemingly indifferent to religion, they encounter at least two kinds of students. Some are interested in questioning, probing, experimenting, and perhaps changing the world. Others seem to want authoritative answers, small groups, Bible studies, religious things. Because most college chaplains are themselves at Fowler's fourth stage, they have equated their faith perspective with the end of human development to which young adults (and the rest of the church) should grow.

These chaplains (including me) hoped that students would move from a religion dependent on parents to a more personally understood and integrated faith. Would probing questions stimulate growth or drive the student away? Would a supportive community provide the secure base for courageous exploration or encourage a dependence on group consensus?

The new faith development theories of Fowler and others seemed to offer a perspective for understanding particular ways in which students hold their faith and what they might need to move to integration of meaning at a higher level of complexity. For example, it seems that many students are at stage three, the *synthetic-conventional* stage described by Fowler; if we could make them more aware of the conflicts between the various authorities in their lives, we might move them into the more reflexive, individually articulated faith of stage four. As faith development theory was presented to campus ministers, the question most frequently asked was, What can we do to move people along?

In addressing this question, I am indebted in particular to the "Faith Development in Campus Ministry" working group that met periodically at Bowling Green State University in the early 1980s. That group spent some time discussing theological and ethical issues related to the use of faith development theory and the end desired by such use. Educators and counselors may wholeheartedly base their work on the proposition that more differentiated functioning is their goal for the individual, and a campus pastor may share that goal. However, the pastor is also committed to minister to people where they are. The pastor is rooted in a particular religious tradition, a particular view of human salvation, and a particular vision of the Kingdom. Thus the goal of the campus pastor is not always simply to move people to presumedly higher levels of functioning. Participants in the group wrestled with this tension, needing to integrate the theory into their view of ministry before proceeding to develop means for assisting faith development.

The group developed several new forms of ministry grounded in the developmental model, and after testing them, reflected on what had been learned. The project resulted in some good continuing ministry that incorporates a faith development perspective, as well as at least three general learnings.

First, the theory is not a quick fix. It will not on its own revitalize campus ministry or congregational ministry to transitional young adults. It is valuable in that it helps clergy distinguish content from process and allows them to see what kinds of ministry may be helpful to people at various points in the faith journey. It provides a way of talking about and clarifying some issues that clergy may have known instinctively. (For project participants, the theory provided a common language.) At the same time, for the theory to be used it must be integrated into personal understanding. The use of personal stories, case studies of students, Biblical references, and exercises in planning all help people integrate the theory with their existing understanding of ministry. In such a process as this, project participants moved beyond a simplistic emphasis on moving people to "higher" stages (a notion foreign to Fowler's theory) to affirm the value of all styles of faith and the need for a comprehensive ministry.

Second, change takes time. In looking at our own faith development and in intentionally nurturing the faith development of others, we were reminded that human growth of any kind is a slow process, fed by many small actions and events.

In addition to theological reasons for abandoning the notion of moving people along, there are some practical reasons learned from this project and other research.

1. As I have listened to people tell their own stories, I have noted that movement from one style of faith to another was generally triggered by a critical incident that had nothing to do with an intentional act of ministry. However, many different forms of ministry were recalled that had sustained individuals at each stage.

2. The data cited by Fowler and Loevinger indicate that many adults spend their lives equilibrated at stage three. Observation and narrative data support a view that for the most part these are mature, faithful, productive people. There are many

young adults with faith at this stage, and they are not necessarily immature, unconcerned, or unfaithful.

3. When faith development between stages does occur, it is,
   noted above, a slow process. "Helping a person move" from
   one stage to another, if meant literally, might well mean having contact with that individual over a period of eight years.
4. It is not easy to determine where a person is developmen-
   tally,and acts of education and ministry usually are carried out
   with groups that are in different stages. Fortunately there is
   some evidence that people will self-select the kinds of groups
   and resources they need at any given point.

Although we cannot move others through stages of faith, we can
be available to minister to them at each stage. The Bible says, "One
planted, another watered, but God gave the increase." We can identify some of the elements that nurture people at each stage, and the
general conditions that the congregation needs to exhibit to be useful to people in the early adult transition.

Many of the traditional forms of ministry work well to support
persons in the process of faith development, and we will look more
in detail at what to do in Chapter IV. Here we can take a general
look at what the congregation can do to support the faith of young
adults, particularly those in the early adult transition.

First, be there. In some of our studies of young adults seventeen
to twenty-five years old, we identified about 50 percent of the population as "happy nonaffiliators." These don't have anything against
the church, might want to see a minister if sick or in serious trou-
ble, and consider themselves believers but don't think about faith
much. Many engage in prayer or other religious practices, and
might attend on high holy days, but basically they are "believers
without belonging." They simply don't feel a need to participate,
but an important part of their world would be gone if the church
disappeared. The attitude is like that of the young person who says
to parents, "I'm leaving home, but don't sell the house."

Second, affirm the questions, and the questioner. For those in
the midst of searching, the questions are the truth and their continuing to live the questions is, as Westerhoff implies, a form of faith.
Even a brief encounter at this point can change an entire life.

Third, provide mentors and peers. All the studies point to the
need young adults have to be significantly engaged with believing
and believable adults. Further, associations with peers are necessary
for challenge, support, and explorations of intimacy in various
forms.

Finally, believe—in real and vibrant ways. Myron Bloy, in a study of congregations near campuses, says no congregation that is not a "palpable manifestation of the new creation" can attract the spiritual seekers of this age. In short, for those seeking some grounding to risk their lives on, it has to be authentic and offer hope for the future.

The developmental viewpoint is an ancient and recurring way of understanding human life, and many examples can be found in art and literature. One ancient Eastern description of the developmental path speaks of the four ages of life as "child," "student," "householder," and "forest journey." The student stage was understood as extending beyond any formal schooling to describe the whole period of exploration, apprenticeship, or traveling that might occur before the young person assumed full householder responsibilities. An echo of this use of the word *student* may be seen in the European or Asian model of student movements, which are likely to include an age range from fifteen to thirty-five. Incidentally, student movements and organizations on that model are more effective than those more age-segregated forms found in the United States because young people learn leadership skills from peers within the organization. This broader understanding of the student stage is very comparable to what we are coming to describe as young adulthood, extending beyond the confines of the traditional college years.

Perhaps when social and economic conditions are right it is possible to compress much of the development of the young adult period into a shorter time frame. There have been times when residential colleges, monastic orders, and military institutions did an effective job of formation in a few years. One notes that those are total environments, and it may be that to work most effectively, such institutions need to be able to control action and information access, as cults attempt to do. But even in a less restrictive form, residential institutions do work, and on a small scale there have been some effective attempts at residential settings for ministry with peers and mentors. Still, some social expectation that forces the young person into the setting helps. I note that twenty-eight-day residential treatment programs for substance abuse have been the institutions through which many of our young adults have grown most in recent years.

In the past half century, many institutions have failed to form young adults in the ways intended. The United States Army did not prepare young men to face brainwashing in Korea, Roman Catholic schools and orders failed to inspire the energies of the young after the 1950s, college educators of the Atlantic alliance worry about the failure to transmit values to the successor generation. And on the other side of the wall, all the mechanisms of state schools, repression, and media control failed to win the conviction of the young for the communist system.

Some time back, Erikson observed that wholistic as well as totalitarian visions appeal to the ideological mind of youth. We could say that the only institution of any scale that might serve as a counterindicator to the trend of failing formation noted above is the Peace Corps; for all its limitations, it does seem to continue to challenge, form, and support a dream in those who participate.

It may be simply that the information age has undermined the ability of institutions to focus the energies of the transition, but I suspect that behind a failure of institutions is a failure of vision. Despite all the mechanisms at its disposal, state communism is an economic and social failure. It is not a vision that can sustain human life, and neither is the consumerist notion that "the one who dies with the most toys wins."

The language of human development has become pervasive in the late twentieth century. Therapists, educators, clergy, and ordinary people all speak of development, stages, transitions, journey, even pilgrimage. One needs to ask, To what? As someone has said, "There must be more to life than raising children to the point where they say, 'There must be more to life.'" We may be approaching a time when the dominant metaphor shifts. John Donne points out that for the figure on pilgrimage, "above" as well as horizon represents the transcendent boundary.

Young adults need to form or latch onto a sustaining vision of life, but they can only do that in interaction with believing and believable adults. "Faith is caught, not taught" is an old and true saying. Children learn the operative values of their parents and form new values in interaction with committed persons. Extensive research shows religion is not transmitted in schools unless they are believing communities. No matter what mechanisms are in place, no institution can transmit or form faith in young adults unless the grounding faith of the institution is believed, believable, lived, and engaging the future. This obviously has profound implications for the church, and we have seen that even at the level of individual congregations, where there is a "palpable manifestation of the new creation," young adults are attracted, involved, and transformed.

However, it is possible to make a significant difference in the lives of young adults even without changing the whole institution. Because they are in a transitional period, small inputs—even one weekend retreat—can make a lifelong difference. Work camps with good mentors and disciplined reflection continue to change lives, and there have been several attempts to import the work-camp model into life within the young adult's normal setting. At the Washington Cathedral, small groups of young adults working in the city live together and reflect together with staff from the cathedral. In the Archdiocese of Seattle, young Roman Catholics drawn to religious vocations continue in secular employment while they reflect regularly on the meaning of vocation with peers and mentors in the Ministerial Development Program.

Finally, even one individual can make a profound difference. William Glasser in *The Identity Society* says that "Involvement with at least one successful person is a requirement for growing up successfully, maintaining success, or changing from failure to success." For young adults in transition, even a brief encounter can make a great deal of difference. When I was first a campus minister, I was confused because sometimes students would come in with a serious problem, talk intensely, and then leave, never to be seen. It was only in time that I began to meet up with such students after the passage of years, at which time many recalled intensely how important their encounter with me had been. I came to discover that students frequently needed only to "touch base" with someone believing in them to renew their own confidence. Such is the adult role of the guarantor as described by Erikson.

Young adults who live in a community may seek out a known pastor in times of crisis even though they are not otherwise involved in worship or church activities. However, pastors themselves often do not grasp the importance of this pastoral activity and generally it is unseen and undervalued by the congregation. When the pastor leaves, the contact between young adults and the congregation is usually broken. One lay adult group was having difficulty identifying young adults related to the congregation; a woman said, "we lost contact with our young people when we hired a seminarian to look after the senior high group." No member of the congregation had significant contact with those young people.

Attention needs to be given to enabling adults to be available as guarantors and supporting them within the community of faith. It is a benefit to older adults to be involved in a ministry of care for the next generation and to have their own lives enriched by the searching faith of young adults. Clergy can provide only the role model of "professional Christian" while lay people can demonstrate to young adults the rich variety of ways in which faith expresses itself in life. Finally, more one-to-one intergenerational contact may lead eventually to changes within congregational life which will redefine the "membership contract" with young adults in such a way that the independent, transitional, searching years can be affirmed, celebrated, and encouraged by the congregation.

In 1989, the William T. Grant foundation conducted a study of the then eighteen to twenty-four-year-old generation, the "baby-busters." this latest report reinforces again what has been concluded about this age group in the past. "American Youth: A Statistical Snapshot," concludes with two suggestions:

—"Enchance the quality of youth and adult relationships;" and,
—"Extend community supports and opportunities for service to all young people.

CHAPTER III

Why and When Young Adults Seek the Church

It would be nice to be able to say that young people are raised in the church, go through a time of questioning and experimentation, and then return to the fold, secure in their committed faith. Looking at the overall pattern of past data, something like that seems to happen. Many young adults discover or return to church involvement between ages twenty-five and thirty-five, but that doesn't happen automatically, and we can't say certainly that future young adults will do so. At present, the average age of return is around twenty-six or twenty-seven, but the process of testing and involvement can take three or four years. Their process of returning looks very much like the *probing commitment* described by Sharon Parks: young adults appear to be testing both themselves and the congregations they seek out. We could say that a majority come seeking commitment rather than as a result of commitment. In any case, church-finding and churchgoing are phenomena that are determined by multiple factors and about which people are generally rather inarticulate.

When we first started interviewing parish clergy about their ministries with college students and others in the early adult transition, we found a commonly expressed attitude; as one pastor put it, "We don't see many people that age. They drop out, but they'll come back when they're thirty." that comment led to The Alban Institute's "Thirty Plus Ministry Project," an attempt to find out if the statement is true, and if so, why people come back, what they are looking for, and what keeps them coming back? We conducted a series of interviews with people in the age range from twenty-five to forty, mostly people who had found their way into one of twenty-eight churches of various denominations around the country. Our sample included a large number of people who at one time had not been attending church and later had made a decision to join. (Our sample was not

randomly drawn, but represented a selected cross section of returnees. Subsequent national statistical samples, randomly drawn, have
verified both that returning is common and that it occurs at the average age cited here.)

The following story is an excerpt from one of a hundred stories
of people now active in congregational life. Although unique, it il-
lustrates some common factors. In interview quotations in this
chapter, names and minor details sometimes have been changed to
protect people's privacy, but the words are taken directly from interviews.)

Ruth's Story

"Well, in high school my father still drove us to church on Sunday.
My mom never went. My mother and father ended up, you know,
really fighting before we'd end up going to church, and as soon as
we were walking out the door it was picked up where it was
dropped off. I remember thinking that it was just very bad of us to
even go into church and the church was very, very large . . . we
went there and it was like a means of getting out of the house-
hold—to have some peace and quiet—but I really didn't get a connection there.

"Immediately after high school I started working and I moved
here, moved in with four girls from my hometown. One girl was
semireligious but she was a very shy person. None of us had cars
and it seemed like none of us were really interested in locating a
church. About a month after I arrived in town . . . it was sheer party-
time, and I partied. I didn't think twice about church.

"Probably one of the first impacts of the church came when my
older sister died and I think it was that time when I probably really
sat down and said, you know, said to God—'Now look, haven't you
hit us with enough problems.'

"I had already gone through—ah, heck—a very religious experience coming out of my accident. I was taking a trip on my motorcy-
cle and I had an accident. The car I was passing was a small-town
doctor and he kept me from bleeding to death right there! It so
happened that a state policeman passed me going the opposite direction and he got an ambulance and got me to the hospital where
there was a neurological surgeon on emergency duty at the time. I
did have an experience with death. I did the . . . you know . . . tun-
nel vision, the white figure at the end, voices . . . I did have that,
which scared me when I was being wheeled into the emergency
room. I remember hearing someone scream and then realizing it

was myself . . . a Catholic priest was giving me last rites. I truly believed and do to this day that if he would have been able to finish it that I would have died right then . . . I felt that God was saying to me that I was heading in the wrong direction, that He was going to give me another chance, but what I needed to do was to take a 180-degree turn and start walking and do it and so that was my transition."

Interviewer: "How old were you when that occurred?"

Ruth: "Twenty-three."

Interviewer: "What did you do with that attitude when you got out of the hospital?"

Ruth: "Well, the first thing I did was started sending money to the Christian Children's Fund—it's the very first thing I did. The next thing I did was I totally reevaluated my moral standards, I reevaluated the type of people I was hanging around with. I became much more earnest in my profession. . . . it took me about three years. I found the type of people I hung around with much more quiet and more serious-minded. As soon as I was able to get around to it the very first thing I did was to take TM. And I found that that really fulfilled a need I was looking for before the accident. . . . Basically those first three years I was in and out of hospitals a lot. My physical therapist turned out to be very Catholic. This little old lady used to talk to me about the Catholic church . . . it was kind of a soothing effect on me but I think basically I was into rebuilding my body, putting weight back on and starting to get on. I found my stubbornness came through . . . it took me a long time to get my head together . . . I found I had become a philosopher type saying, 'Well, God doesn't give you more crosses than you can bear.' I started doing that, and I also found that I was—still am at times—a good resource and a good example for people at times of tribulation."

Interviewer: "What was it that brought you here, to this congregation?"

Ruth: "Well, I was working in the bar and this guy came up, good-looking guy, came in and I was singing at the jukebox and he said, 'You've got a pretty good voice.' And I said, 'Yeah, and I really like singing with the jukebox, the only problem is you can't harmonize with the jukebox and there's not that many good singers around here.' And he said, 'Well, we've got a good choir down on Indiana, if you want to come over and join us.' And I said, 'Where is it?' He said 'St. Mark's Church.' And I said, 'Ah, the roof'll fall in!' "

"It took him—he never really pushed me—and I guess I was dating him about three months before I finally showed up at church one Thursday evening for choir rehearsal . . . hiding behind this guy, I was like a kid. So, finally, the choir director insisted that if I was going to come to rehearsals that I had to come to church on Sundays. I finally showed up at church on a Sunday and I decided it wasn't so bad—so I came the next Sunday. Then I realized that the oboe player that played the week that the singers weren't singing—I'd missed that. And the dance company would come, and I'd missed that! Oh, I missed all this neat stuff. That's when I started coming here.

"I was a very angry person for a while and I went to a parish planning conference. The issue they were covering was single parents, and like, social activities and getting them involved in meeting other people. And that Sunday morning after a whole weekend of listening to this stuff . . . they said, 'Anyone else have anything else to say?' I stood up and I said, 'This looks like a social club, just like the bars that I hang around in. Where is the religion in the church?' And that's when people started talking. . . . I still kind of stood back and watched and listened to lots of it closely and after about two years I decided, well, I could get into a class. . . .'"

Ruth recalls that during this period of peripheral involvement with the congregation, the pastor visited her in the hospital one Christmas Eve. She says, "He seemed like a person—someone I could really relate to—he really listened to you and he seemed to be very quiet and understanding and caring and yet not pushy. I found that I'd throw test questions at him and he would just turn, just hand it back to me, saying, 'What do you think?'" Basically though, Ruth says it was her faith that kept her involved with the church.

"I believed. I believed that at that point this was my way of getting in touch with God . . . I felt as though this was my contribution, this was talking to my God. Then I realized that here whatever He looks like to you is fine, doesn't make any difference. Like there are Jewish people here, Baptists, a lot of Catholics—who would believe that! . . . I didn't take communion—maybe I'd been coming to church a year before I took communion—I got tricked into it. . . . I just never took communion because that was sacrilegious. And then, one of the guys in the choir invited me to be a lay servant and so I went up there forgetting the fact that the lay servants are the first people to receive communion. Inside I said, 'Oh no, you can't refuse now!' So I said, 'Well, I did it once, it's OK I guess.'"

Ruth made a decision to join the church at this point, talked with the pastor, took membership classes, and has subsequently become very active around the congregation and a member of the church's governing board. She goes on to describe some of the impact of the church on her life.

"I find it easier to discuss God and my beliefs. I find I have a tendency to choose close friends who are a part of or willing to get involved in this community. ... [The church] offers a lot of courses that are very beneficial. I took a women's missions course and found that a lot of problems that I face in life—that I think are my own—are shared. ... I would say that most of my social energies are directed to here. You'll find me involved in almost all aspects of the church. I'm a great list-maker and organizer and systems-establisher ... I spend a lot of time here ... I'm responsible ... I'm definitely a very integral part of this congregation and I know—as I get older—that this is my family, that I won't be abandoned or lost or forgotten. ... I used to be one of the most vocal, angry people you ever met. I think I see myself softening as a person and I see myself as becoming the person I am ... Well, there's the communion and the service. It's like an elevated place away from, you might say, my worries and cares of everyday life ... I absolutely believe that when I take communion, right when I take communion—that's probably the second closest time that I can be with God and really talk—that's when I'm being most spiritual."

Interviewer: "Do you consider yourself a religious person?"

Ruth: "Well, I truly believe in God. I truly believe that I'm much more spiritual than I've ever been before. I absolutely miss this—I feel a lacking when I don't show up for church. I mean there's that one moment when I don't get to have my conversation with God. ... So when you look at that I would say, yes, I'm religious—but when you look at the fact that I do get drunk and I do curse and I do have sex and I do yell and scream and I do hurt people's feelings—I do commit sins—I don't go around professing God, save the world, and pushing God on people. So when I look at that part of it, I'd say I'm not religious, but I find that the songs that I sing at work or in the home—all of them are religious songs, with rare exceptions. ... I think that my person, my person on the whole is religious."

A Common Journey

While Ruth's story is more dramatic than most, it has a number of elements in common with the religious journeys of other young adults, both in its telling and in its content. In the course of conducting interviews, we asked people to draw a time line of their involvement with the church, going up when they were more involved and down when they were less involved. There were many stories and patterns, and some did not extend beyond the midtwenties. But putting them all together, the following pattern emerged as a common story.

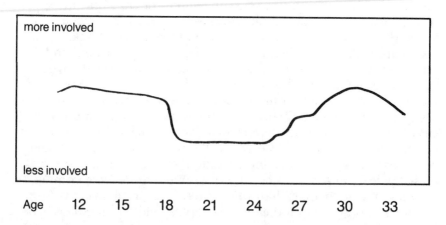

The major steps on this common journey include

1. *Church involvement as a child,* continuing through high school when there was a church-related peer group. Confirmation, adult baptism, or other act of adult membership is common in the years between ages ten and fourteen.

2. *Dropping out* or greatly reduced church attendance beginning between the ages of ten and twenty-seven, most commonly beginning at age eighteen.

3. *A period of noninvolvement,* lasting an average of eight years. Most young adults who are not actively involved with the church continue to be believers, but some are very critical of religious institutions.

4. A *return* to church involvement, at an average age of twenty-six or twenty-seven. The process of return may take several years and is often not a reaffiliation with the same congregation or denomination.

5. Often a *period of very active church involvement* follows after a new congregational affiliation is established, which sometimes is followed by burnout.

The general schema is one of being exposed to a religious environment as a child, dropping out of congregational life, and experiencing a transition event or events, as well as other factors, that lead to reinvolvement.

A religious background. As a child, Ruth was exposed to religion, as are most Americans, according to Gallup poll data. All but a few of the people we talked with had some exposure to religion, which was often remembered with mixed feelings. A number of people had attended church or Sunday school on their own without parental support. This and the absence of religious observance in the childhood homes of many surprised us because parental example is generally regarded as an important predictor of later attendance patterns as adults. It is often said that "just dropping kids off at Sunday school doesn't do any good," but doing so may have greater impact on children than has been credited.

It is the memories of *people* from childhood that is most salient. One man said, "I had a lot of respect for those people, I guess that's what sticks in my mind—it's hard to put into concrete terms. . . . You have got to get to know your Sunday school teacher—and I had some great ones, at least I thought I did. It's not that they knew all the rules, but they just had a way of doing things that made a lot of sense. And when you get older, you realize that they had a value system and dedication to certain principles that kept them on an even keel."

However, the presence of strong religious figures in early life is not a sure predictor of later behavior. One woman described how her own religious interest had been kindled by a strict Pentecostal grandmother whom she had visited during the summers of her childhood. Later, speaking of why some acquaintances were not churchgoers, she said, "Well, my twin sister is a good example. We've talked about it some, and she was really turned off to religion by my grandmother. My sister hated it that she wouldn't let us go to the movies or dances or anything."

A dropout period. Sixty percent of those whom we individually interviewed had gone through a period of at least two years in which they did not attend church except for special occasions. The age at which people most commonly drop out of church involvement, and the average age at dropping out in our sample, is eighteen. One dropped out as early as age ten and one as late as age twenty-seven, but 85 percent dropped out between the ages of thirteen and twenty-three.

Although many of the people we interviewed individually were not dropouts or unchurched in the precise sense of having been nonattenders for at least two years, most had experienced a period of greatly reduced church involvement. The ages of reduced involvement were similar to those given above for dropouts. Overall, we might reasonably assume that at least half the persons in this age range have been unchurched for a period of at least two years, and perhaps as high as 80 percent have shared the experience by having a period of significantly reduced church involvement.

These were all *developmental dropouts*—that is, they stopped going to church when their parents stopped making them go, when they moved away from home, when they graduated from school or college, or, as one male put it, "when I got interested in cars and girls." Although many were critical of some part of their church experience, only one of those responding cited a particular instance of conflict with the church as a reason for leaving. In contrast, one eighty-year-old woman from a control group reported that she had dropped out at sixty-eight, and she wrote in, "It had nothing to do with age!"

Other research (particularly the work of John Savage in *The Bored and Apathetic Church Member*) has indicated that older church members who drop out are likely to have done so in response to some conflict in or with their congregation or in their own lives. That research suggests that these older dropouts may be reconciled to the church if appropriately visited within six weeks, otherwise their unchurched status may become permanent.

In contrast, few of the developmental dropouts we talked with were hostile toward the church. They generally did not think about the church during their period of nonattendance. In some cases they thought about it but they "were busy" or judged the church to be irrelevant to their lives. When asked why she had returned to church attendance after a twenty-year lapse, one woman replied, "Oh well, I'd always liked the church!" Another woman who didn't attend for seven years said:

"When I think about why not, I'm not real sure. At that point I very much believed I didn't need it . . . there was a period [when] I was angry at everything . . . the church didn't offer a great deal . . . when I went back, I couldn't really remember why I'd stopped."

The dropouts we talked with had stayed away from church from two to twenty years, with an average of eight and one-half years of noninvolvement except for special occasions.

A transition event. People frequently reported a major change in their lives that preceded their reinvolvement with church life, but the connection between those two events was seldom immediate or direct. We did not hear stories of people seeking out the church at the point of crisis or change. Those whose reentry was connected with a transition event seemed to become involved with the church in the process of restructuring and reordering their lives after the crisis. In Ruth's story above, she did not seek out the church or religious representatives immediately following her accident, but the change in her life following the accident made her open to church involvement three years later. Similarly, several people became involved with a congregation in the process of restructuring their lives following a divorce, but did not seek the church at the point of crisis.

In some cases, the connection between a crisis event and church involvement had not been considered by the individual sharing the story. For example, Karen told of her gradual church involvement that she dated to a good Easter service she had attended with a friend four years earlier. Later in the interview, after reporting on factors that drew her into the life of the congregation, and on many changes in her work and love life, she said, "In that period also, my father had died . . . let me see, it predates my involvement here, . . . yes, it was just immediately before that Eastertime."

We might attribute her openness to the church at that point to the impact of her father's death, but it is not a connection she made at the time nor was the death a crisis in which she consciously sought some special ministry from the church. A series of experiences with the church over a year and a half subsequent to that Easter drew Karen into meaningful participation. Perhaps frequently neither the pastor greeting a visitor nor the visitor understand what has brought that person to church now.

Looking retrospectively at individual lives, we can easily find transition points that have preceded church involvement because there are so many such points. Life during an individual's twenties and thirties is subject to many changes. On a list of thirty-eight significant life events our sample averaged over two events per year throughout the late twenties and thirties. Changes most frequently reported were moving to a new home, change of job, added volunteer activities, period of depression, birth of a child, moving to a new community, and new responsibilities at work.

There were many other endings, beginnings, conflicts, and changes. Therefore, we can say that a return to church involvement was preceded by a life transition in most cases, but this may not be the most significant factor to consider. A life transition is certainly not a sufficient condition for a return to active church participation, and even if it is a necessary condition, it is one easily met because there are so many life changes.

In listening to stories of young adults, one glimpses events that may have opened the search for meaning—Ruth's accident, the death of Karen's father, Bill's experience of first holding his newborn daughter. However, conversions through intellectual search or religious experience are notable for their absence as events preceding entry into congregational life. That is, the stories we heard are not about a conversion experience or resolution of a crisis of faith.

This is true despite there being those who were intellectually curious and the presence of many religious experiences, in the sense of moments people felt especially close to a transcendent reality, as in Ruth's account of her accident. One respondent said that an awareness of God's presence is what sustained her long absence from congregational life.

The Transition to Involvement

Witnesses and facilitating people. Those whose journeys led them to involvement in a congregation often encountered both witnesses to a faith and facilitating persons who introduced them to a congregation. In Ruth's story, her physical therapist served as a witness to and reminder of the religion of her childhood. Reviewing his story, Jack described an encounter with a Mennonite farmer:

"I was in the middle of nowhere and two flats. . . . He came out, took two brand new tires out of his garage, took them to my car, jacked the car up—wouldn't let me touch it. He took the tires off and threw them in the back of the truck and we went to another farm, changed the tires, put his new tires on my rims, put them on for me. . . . Well, I wanted to give him my driver's license or my license plus a twenty-dollar bill just for the help, and he said, 'No, no, when you get tires, you just bring them back.'

"Never knew me. Never seen me before in his life. Well, I didn't get back fast enough for me. He knew I'd be back. But he was open, he showed me what I was looking for, and I didn't know it at that time either. But he had, right there he was right in front of me, God's love was being showed to me right there. I'd driven by this church for years, and I always wondered, What's a Mennonite? Some kind of new truck or something?"

Juan, a social activist, said:

"My boss at work is a Catholic, a practicing, devout Catholic, and I see him as a person who's very honest, very intelligent, very compassionate, and believes in many of the same things I believe in, yet is able to be a practicing Catholic and be proud of the fact. I've had many discussions with him. . . . He's always been very frank and reassuring with me."

Quite a few people noted that they had been invited to church at times when they were not ready and had ignored the invitation. The invitation in itself was not enough, but at a time of readiness there was often a person who facilitated their actual involvement in congregational life—most frequently a spouse, fiancee, or friend.

These people were frequently remembered as young adults described how and when they got involved in congregational life.

"Attended church on a nonregular basis. Would find other things to do on Sunday rather than go to church. Two friends visited my house one evening whom I thought a lot of and invited us to come to church, I could see how happy he was and what his church meant to him" (age twenty-seven).

—"Looking for 'something' other than material gratification. Wanted a church I could relate to and with. Some friends told us about St. M's and said it was progressive, not staid, and young" (age thirty-one).

—"I was about twenty-five years old when I became involved in this congregation at the suggestion and initiation of my wife."

—"We needed a steady or even influence in our life. We were ready to settle down. We enjoyed the people connected with this church, and David [the minister] was the only one who called on us when we were new in town" (age thirty).

The role of the minister. Sometimes the minister is a facilitating person, like David, who called on the newcomers in town. Or a minister met in the community may be a witness:

"Father Dan—I can't remember his last name—he was from the church here. He was involved with Fair Share, a community organization which I'm a part of. . . . and I saw that at least through his eyes Christianity and the church is supposed to care and supposed to be involved in the community, and I could never be involved if I didn't feel that that was the case. . . . Since then, I've met other people, particularly Brother Val . . . , who I've had lots of discussions with on the church in the last year and a half because I love and respect him deeply, and I know his commitment to people."

In almost every congregation visited there was a group of people who had been brought into the congregation directly through the pastor's contacts in the community. Often they were similar to the pastor in age, interests, and lifestyle. For example, in one church co-pastored by a husband and wife, there had gathered a number of young couples who shared a lifestyle of dual careers and shared parenting.

In every congregation, even those that tried to downplay the special status of the ordained minister, the pastor was a key figure for those entering congregational life. Liking the minister is frequently cited as a reason for affiliating with a congregation. From what people say, we gather that the pastor's preaching, interpersonal style, manner of conducting services, and manner of life are all evaluated, often unconsciously, by visitors. Not infrequently the minister, as a representative of faith, is tested. As Ruth said, "I'd throw test questions at him." Later she said, "If he would have gotten angry with me at that point, I would have left."

Until newcomers get to know other people, the ordained minister may be the only member of the congregation whom they know and are known by. The pastor is a key "gatekeeper," the one who invites newcomers to participate in other activities and lets them in.

Moving into activities. Discovering a proper orbit of involvement in congregational life can take several years. Some people take two to three years to join a congregation, during which they may be involved in a parish school, community project, or choir, or as a Sunday school teacher, while still evaluating their commitment. Others may be most comfortable simply attending services, and perhaps gaining a lot from that activity, like one person who said, "I sat back and 'watched the action' for two years. I especially enjoyed hearing the sermons by Rev. H—always seemed to tie in with my inner turmoil and turmoil around me."

Different people can have different experiences in the same congregation, as these two experiences from the same congregation illustrate:

"My only involvement for the first two-and-a-half years was to attend the Bethel Bible Series ... we became more involved after attending the Marriage Encounter ... it was hard to meet people here until then."

"You get instantly involved here—they ask you to do everything. I was inundated with requests for my time."

Of course, perhaps congregations respond differently to some people than others, finding some "more desirable." And some people need to hold back, to test their own commitment, to not be rushed, while others need a place to be intensely involved. One person said, "I'm basically a doer. I like to get involved rather than sit back and watch, so I offered to help usher, sing in the choir, teach adult Bible study classes."

Most people are not quite so confident in a new environment, and for them, *being asked personally* was the important key to their finding an appropriate involvement.

Overinvolvement. For a surprisingly high number of the people we talked with, initial involvement led to overinvolvement. The following comments from people in their late twenties and thirties were typical:

"At first I became too involved. When someone would ask me to help, I always helped if I could. I had a full-time job, and it was hard to do so many things for the church. I was going to meetings at least four to five times a week. It was too much."

"I got involved in too many things and had to spread myself too thin … it got so my work at school suffered and my relationship with my husband did too. I had no free time to even read a book. I had to leave guilt feelings behind and say no to doing different jobs."

"I feel that I am too much involved. Whenever something becomes too important, you begin not to have as much fun. A lot of money has been spent on me to help me learn the 'new role of laity in the church.' I feel that I must work to put the money 'back.' But I look forward to the day that I can go to a church function and not have to take something or clean up."

Persons who got very involved in church activity or assumed some office in the congregation frequently experienced not only burnout but also disillusionment as they discovered human beings and human failings in an institution they had idealized:

"People's un-Christian-ness in get-togethers greatly surprised me."

"As I began to reach out, I discovered there was a clique of people who ran everything, and it was very difficult to break in. I was disappointed, felt a bit unwelcome."

"I became disillusioned with the church because I found it was run as a corporation with all the politics involved."

We expect that some people we did not talk with dropped out again at the point of disillusion, but for others the disenchantment became an occasion for spiritual growth, as indicated by the following comment:

"Crisis came when priests were found to be living most negative lives—obviously. Began to see how human they were. A lot of politics were involved. Hierarchy lost credibility for me. I learned to see beyond these things—that faith (mine) depended on other things, not the hierarchy."

Aids to Involvement

The journey to reinvolvement described above is a common story but not the only one. Some people never totally drop out of church participation. Some go away for a few years and return to their home community and congregation. Many move and seek out a congregation in a new community. Although the experience of seeking a church could occur at any age, the comments included here are from young adults, and this analysis reflects their experience. Whatever the story, as people come in contact with a congregation certain elements help them become more involved. Among these are the congregation's atmosphere, clergy, personal relationships, invitations to involvement, and program.

Atmosphere. "I can feel God's presence when I come here—and peace."

People may often judge a church by a number of intangible and nonverbal signals. Even before they first walk in the door, visitors have drawn some conclusions about a congregation from the church's building, signs, upkeep, and other externals. Once inside, they gather further "vibrations" from the building, manner in which the service is conducted, style in which people relate to one another, and the contests of service and sermon. Many people are looking for a congregation whose style is familiar to them from childhood. Overall, the terms people most often used to describe a congregation they liked were

—open and accessible
—conducive to spiritual growth
—sincere and honest
—friendly and informal
—has an "alive" feeling, exuberance

The clergy. The pastor may be the newcomer's first contact with the congregation and is often the only person whose words are heard at a worship service. Those who have been around a church for a while will often stay even if they don't like the pastor, but few newcomers will join a church unless they have a positive feeling toward the pastor. Judgments are made about a clergyperson on the basis of both personal and professional skills. One group that felt very positive about their pastor quickly listed the following characteristics about him:

—related to everyday life
—easy to talk to; relaxing, comfortable
—his wife is easy to talk to
—wife and pastor are our friends—more than just a minister
—well educated, easy for us to relate to him
—runs an open administration
—honest, self-confident, makes us feel confident in ourselves

The sermon is particularly important. The positive comment most frequently made about sermons is, He relates the message to everyday life. That connection between the everyday and the religious realms is what people seem to be looking for most often from the church.

Personal relationships. Only a few people we talked with initially sought out the church as a place to make friends, but the friendliness of the people and the quality of their relationships at church often became a primary attraction of the congregation. People said:

"I met people who were totally accepting of me. They did not demand that I be here or there but just let me be wherever I felt comfortable."

"At first I was attending church on Sunday. The ambiance of the community and the friendly and sincere attitude of the congregation and parish staff helped me get more involved."

"The members wove a net for me with small kindnesses."

Knowing someone, being greeted by name, feeling accepted, and feeling as though one fit in were all important for people being drawn into church involvement.

Invitations to involvement and program. For many, the next step was being personally asked to do some task that helped them become further involved in the congregation's life. Thus people said:

"I began to get involved when asked about teaching in the Sunday school of religion. . . ."

"I was personally asked to get involved. . . ."

People appreciated being asked because it made them feel welcomed, known, needed, and valued. At the same time, others said that they appreciated being allowed to say no to tasks. The following comment reflects the feelings expressed by a number of people:

"Ron helped me get involved because of his willingness to let people be themselves and to do what they want to do, not what he thinks they should do."

Although the worship, clergy, people, and overall atmosphere were the most critical elements in most people's evaluation of the church, for some people specific programs helped involvement. Choirs were a major way for some to get introduced to and involved in a church. A woman said:

"My husband and I were out of school and no longer were singing in the choirs. We both really missed that so we joined the choir at church and attended every week. Since we were in church regularly twice a week, we were more aware of other activities and began attending some of those."

The singing itself was important for many people other than those who join the choir. Thus one respondent said:

"I love to sing and found I no longer felt out of place express-
ing my feelings through songs in church—I've always been too shy
to join a church choir."

Some parents who have been inactive and who may remain so
turn to church-related schools for their children. Where a parish
day school exists, it is a route of entry for young parents, but their
activity usually centers more in the school than in the church. Thus
one woman said:

The fact that my oldest child was in school brought with it the
necessity to become involved in school-related affairs, more than
parish-related affairs."

But the interest of young parents in a church-related school may
lead to other involvements. In some places, parents must speak to
church staff when they register their children and on other occasions. Some churches design special worship services for school
children and parents, particularly at holiday times. One parent said:

"Our children were the primary reason for initial involvement.
Once they entered the parish school we became involved in school
board activities. This reinforced regular church attendance and led
to increased involvement in social and spiritual activities. Our ac-
quaintance with the current and previous pastors and sisters has all
supported and increased involvement."

In congregations without a parish day school, some parents
were drawn to a Sunday school, a preschool program, or a program
of music instruction for children. Generally we found that parents
did not stay involved solely for the sake of the children, but in
some cases of exceptionally good Sunday schools the children
brought the parents. In one congregation with a long tradition of
quality Christian education a mother said:

"The Sunday school program was very strong and perceptive. I
liked my girls being taught by a couple. My oldest has not missed a
Sunday in eighteen months. She will give me a list of members to
call to arrange rides if I am unable to take her. Caring was always
evident; judgment was not present."

Teaching Sunday school brought some parents, first out of obligation and then through interest, as they learned from their studies.
A scattering of other education programs, activities, and retreats
helped individual transitions into church life as the following comments illustrate:

"Became involved in nursery program, teaching Sunday school
somewhat."

"Developed friendships with people around my age group. Bas-
ketball and softball teams strongly influenced our social involvement with this church."

"I've gotten involved, in many ways on the sidelines, by teaching Sunday school; it doesn't mean involvement with adults."

"Social activities with other singles. . . ."

"Involvement deepened because of participation in Cursillo. . . ."

"We always liked discussion groups—good way to meet people with similar values."

"Liturgy committee sparked interest in biblical study. . . ."

"Involved in sharing and meal program. . . ."

"The faith-sharing group provided an outlet for discussion and genuine growth in faith."

"Our 'young adults' class provided good lessons and many social occasions."

The following comment sums up several of the factors that helped people get involved:

"First I went on a retreat and dealt with basic faith issues. A lot had happened since I quit the church. The pastor made me feel comfortable. A few thirty-ish people who knew my friend invited us for dinner and encouraged my participation. The liturgies were good: good music, good homilies. Father always had projects for us to work on. I felt useful."

Barriers. "I married a member of another church and attended there for a while, but it was not what I sought in life. Did not feel anything was taking place in that other church—too church-centered. Problems with church schedules, hers and mine, caused some friction at first. Sometimes difficult to attend with a young child to watch. Bigness of church was difficult to overcome. . . ."

Any of the elements that helped involvement could also get in the way if experienced negatively. People were sometimes put off by churches different in size or tradition from their own experience. In some places people judged the atmosphere not conducive to worship, the pastor inept, or the people cold. Some of the negative factors that put off people about the church follow:

—worship service strange
—large financial problems of church
—business or political nature of church
—traditional way of church
—felt resentment of young people
—lack of communication
—difficulty being accepted as a woman
—not very active church
—asked to do too much
—clique of people running everything

—older members prejudiced
—pastor being manipulated by people
—staff emphasis on restraint
—changes in worship
—minister

When the pastor was cited as a problem, there were complaints about boring sermons, poor church administration, and inept or nonexistent pastoral care. Much more frequently, however, there were complaints about worship being different from one's expectations or in general being uninspiring. The most common complaints were about not feeling welcome, or about not fitting into the congregation. One example of this is the common complaint of single persons who felt that many congregations were family-oriented to the point of excluding them.

At least 5 percent of our respondents had experienced some problem regarding the attitudes of parishioners toward children or a deficiency in the programs offered for children. Many others simply identified having very young children as a personal barrier to their participation in church. Frequently people said that they had decreased church participation when their children were infants. Other barriers to participation people identified as their own, rather than the institution's, included the following:

—conflict with partner over church
—own need for space
—personal rebellion, doubts, and fears
—work schedule conflicts

Although respondents owned these barriers as their responsibility, we noted that some congregations helped overcome these barriers by providing good child care for all activities, by making it easy for nonmember partners to attend and participate in their own way, by affirming searching, and by allowing for different styles and times of participation.

Surprises. To speak of people coming back to church may be misleading.

At least half the people interviewed in this study had been nonparticipants for at least two years, and some much longer. The average length of time for which those dropouts had not participated in a church was eight years. During that period they had changed a lot. More than one person indicated that by the time they renewed interest in the church they couldn't remember why they had left.

For others, involvement with a church was a new experience, born out of a new maturity as adults. Even when a person became active as an adult in the same congregation in which he or she had grown up, both the individual and the congregation had changed. It was not a simple case of the same person returning. One young man said:

"My parents were leaders of the parish, so my brother and I had strong examples of service and role models. In my twenties though, having grown up here, some people saw me as the five-year-old I used to be, and that sometimes hampered me in making the contribution to leadership I would have preferred."

In some cases the church had changed. One woman said:

"I was surprised by the new services—find it strange—am not yet comfortable with it."

Others were surprised that the church and its clergy were friendly, not cool as remembered. Several expressed surprise that people could care so much, that the church could be family. Positive surprises were generally the experience of that one-third of the sample who ended up in denominations other than those they were raised in. One said:

"I did not seek out this church; my fiancee was raised in this church so we attended together off and on. I found that I preferred the worship service and intellectual atmosphere to those in the church I was raised in. I enjoy the music, the liturgical service, and the thoughtful, intelligent approach to Christianity."

For both converts and returnees, those who stayed around did so because they were pleased with what they found. As one man said:

"I had left the 'bad news' church (Catholic school fear, guilt, etc.) and came back to the 'good news' church."

Dimensions of Involvement

"Why do you suppose *she* is in church?" Churchgoers, preachers, researchers, all may wonder at times why others go to church. Cynics and folks who themselves don't attend may attribute to churchgoers motives of guilt, habit, fear, or superstition. When asked why they go to church people are frequently inarticulate. They say such things as "Well, it kinda makes my week. I wouldn't feel right if I didn't go." In George Gallup's study of the unchurched American, 48 percent of those who had dropped out and later returned to church participation gave answers in the "Don't know/No answer" category when asked why they had returned to church.

The United States continues to be a nation of churchgoers. Americans are far more likely to attend church than their counterparts in Western Europe, and large majorities of American adults claim that their religious beliefs are important to them. John Pollock, in releasing a study of American values, expressed surprise that the "religious factor" is so strong in shaping American values. He said, "We tried washing out the religious factor ... but it didn't wash out. It equalled or exceeded the age factor."

American religion is a complex mix, and although what people believe is often a major determinant of their action, it may not determine their churchgoing. Churchgoers are somewhat more likely to hold traditional beliefs, but few sharp distinctions exist between churchgoers and nonchurchgoers. In the American understanding, churchgoing is not an essential. Gallup's study, "The Unchurched American," reported that 88 percent of the unchurched and 70 percent of the churched agreed that a person can be a good Christian or Jew without attending church or synagogue. Nearly the same percentage of each group agreed that an individual should arrive at his or her own religious beliefs independent of any churches or synagogues. Still, people go to church. Polls and informal reports both indicate that even the baby-boom dropouts of the sixties have returned to church participation in numbers nearly as great as their parents. The churchgoing rate in the U.S. is now what it was prior to World War II. On an average weekend, 40 percent of adult Americans will attend a house of worship; 60 percent belong to a congregation. Why do they do it? What are they looking for? What keeps them coming back? The responses reported below are from young adults, the group most likely to be looking for a congregation to participate in; and most of the comments came from people between twenty-five and thirty-five years old.

Refreshment and religion. People come to receive religious nurture, to pray, and to belong. People said that they came to church for the *refreshment,* that is, for spiritual refreshment. Here are some of the responses people gave in completing the sentence, "The main reason I go to church is ... :"

—refreshment
—religious refreshment and to see friends
—support, growth, fulfillment
—spiritual uplift and fellowship
—to receive the support and nourishment from God and the community
—faith and fellowship

—for spiritual revitalization
—spiritual growth and fellowship
—spiritual inspiration and fellowship

In addition to those who go to church for spiritual refreshment, uplift, or peace, a number of people attend for guidance or to learn. Quite a few respondents used specifically religious language to explain why they attend church, such as those who said:

—to worship God
—because I love the Lord
—I love God and he commands my worship
—to give thanks
—to practice and fulfill my faith
—to worship God in fellowship with believers

Belonging. A person unfamiliar with our metaphors might assume not only that the church served good refreshments, but also that it had the one building with a furnace. What people who are part of a congregation like best about it is that it is *warm.* Few people we interviewed had sought out the church as a place to make friends or as a way to become involved in community life, but fellowship and a sense of belonging became major reasons why people continued to attend church. What those presently part of a congregation value most is the quality of relationships. Congregations were nearly always described by their members as "warm and friendly" no matter how they might appear to outsiders.

At one level, belonging is part friendship and part clannishness. In one city congregation with a small-group process to integrate members, the pastor says, "No matter what we do, unless newcomers make at least one personal friend, they tend to drop away." In country churches where many people have belonged since childhood, to ask the question, Why are you a member? seems as meaningless as to ask why one is a member of one's family. Every congregation signals its ethnic and class identity by the songs it sings, the food it serves, the language it speaks. On the basis of such clues, people choose congregations in which they feel comfortable and "fit in."

People talk about congregational life in a way that seems to go beyond friendship and clannishness to suggest special qualities of religious belonging. The words *family, community,* and *fellowship* are frequently used to describe the congregation. The church is expected to be a special place, a setting in which there is unconditional acceptance of the individual, inclusiveness and an absence of status distinctions between persons, mutual assistance and an absence of competition, a willingness to take pain and life issues seriously, and loyalty to a transcendent reference. Finding some of these elements can lead to an initial "falling in love" with the congregation; the inevitable discovery that these ideals are not always present leads to disappointment and disillusionment. The tendency to overvalue leads some people in every congregation to make grand claims, such as these:

—Everyone is welcome here.
—I was totally accepted.
—Everybody would come to help out in a crisis.
—We include the whole range from very poor to very rich.

In reality, people do find in the religious congregation an embodiment of certain values, beliefs, and visions of life. A blue-collar former convict finds that he can talk with the mayor at coffee hour. A macho steamfitter discovers it is acceptable to be emotional and hug a friend. A housewife finds her gifts as a leader encouraged. Men talk informally about their problems raising children while selling Christmas trees or waiting for the adult class to start. People are greeted by name and, apparently for once during the week, are valued for themselves and not their skills.

Pastors and other religious leaders often make a distinction between the religious and social goals of congregational activities that many of our respondents did not. As one woman responsible for singles social activities in her church said, "I can't separate the social and the spiritual." A man active in community service and reflective about his personal religious beliefs said, when asked why he attends church:

"The social contact more than anything else, with the people in the church. I get something out of the sermon, but that's not why I come ... mostly the contact ... well, I think that's what God, what religion is all about anyway."

What people said they liked best about their congregation was somewhat different from what had first attracted them. Over 60 percent mentioned some aspect of belonging (friendship; warmth; feeling accepted, welcomed, cared for) when asked what they liked best about the congregation. Only 10 percent mentioned the pastor, and others mentioned the worship, outreach, education, or faith stance of the congregation. As people become more involved in a congregation, the importance of the pastor and other factors that initially attracted them decline as the relationship with other members becomes primary. The fellowship aspect of the church becomes most important to many members in a way that it is hard for outsiders to see or to understand. Therefore, the gap between churched and unchurched becomes greater.

Family. In addition to the desire for religion and a sense of belonging, another set of responses emphasizes a concern for children and family life. Thus some said, "The main reason I go to church is . . . :"

—"to involve my children and for family activities."
—"spiritual support for myself and family."

Although the shape of the family may be changing, four out of five adult Americans consider having a good family life very important, and family holds the highest rank of nineteen social values in Gallup polls. Those whom we interviewed most frequently volunteered "my family" when asked, "What gives your life meaning?" In a similar manner, family was most frequently mentioned in the following sentence completion. "The most important thing in my life right now is . . . :"

—"my family and their growth."
—"my children."
—"my family."
—"my husband and child."
—"raising my children in the best way I can."
—"my family—making ends meet."
—"marriage and motherhood."
—"my wife and daughter's welfare."

The church is seen by many people as an institution supportive of the family through its worship, proclaimed values, instruction of children, and family-oriented activities. Some turn to it for marital aid or support it for the sake of family solidarity, as the following comments about return to church activity illustrate:

"At age twenty-three we were expecting our second child, and we were beginning to lose touch with each other. We both began searching for something we knew was missing."

"My wife was a member of this church, and I started going with her. Plus I wanted to be a good influence on my children." (age thirty-two).

"I was 18 when I met my husband. He was Catholic and at that time my own family did not go to church on a regular basis. I felt that a common religion was one basic a good marriage should have."

Gallup's poll cited above indicates that having "a good family life" is very important for twice as many people as being "active in church or synagogue." It is therefore not surprising to hear that people's decisions about church participation are often determined by their family situation. Our interviews support the findings of other research indicating that marriage is the most frequent cause for switching denominational preference or changing the pattern of religious participation in adulthood. When a couple have a continued conflict about church participation, they often both drop out of participation to avoid the conflict. Several divorced persons were nonparticipants during their married years for such reasons but after divorce felt free to resume church attendance. We assume that many people in this age bracket continue to be nonattenders because their spouses not attend. We know that many in the age-group attend primarily because their spouses do, or in general to support family life.

Some people say they attend to set an example or to provide religious instruction for their children. Although these reasons often provide an initial motivation, most people seem to leave unless they find something for themselves as well. Only a very few mentioned prior training, obligation, or family tradition as chief reasons for their own current church attendance.

Why people don't attend. Although members value the fellowship and the corporate gathering of the church to worship, few view it as essential. All those interviewed would describe themselves as "a person of faith" but many would not describe themselves as "a religious person" because that has negative connotations for them. Several people, particularly younger ones, made a point of saying, "I don't think you have to go to church." When asked about reasons why some of their friends might be unchurched, most respondents answered in terms of negative church experience, lack of church experience, or the absence of internal spark:

—they don't have clear idea of what faith or church is
—bad previous experience with organized religion
—church is to them just ceremony, entertainment
—problems with church's stand on divorce, remarriage, birth control
—turned off at a young age
—see church as a "racket"
—turned off by "evangelism"
—lack of spiritual depth in church
—people don't seem to have a need
—didn't have church background

—don't think about religion
—already feel secure in relation to the Lord—don't need to
  come
—nonbelief, different values
—too busy, work schedule

Church leaders were more likely to attribute nonattendance to laziness, lack of belief, self-centered behavior, or a failure of parents to inculcate a sense of duty. Quite a few lay leaders simply admitted that they had no idea of what might be the needs or issues of the unchurched, or of those persons in their twenties and thirties who occasionally attended church but who were not involved in other congregational activities. We assume that congregational leadership is most commonly drawn from those to whom "belonging" in the congregation is most important. Those persons understandably have difficulty understanding those church participants for whom belonging and church-related activity is of little importance.

How church affects life. What people seek from the church is support for their lives—human support and a transcendent, religious context. One man happy with his congregation wrote:
"We were strengthened by the fellowship—felt wonderful support of our values and lifestyle, childrearing, and social concerns. Uninteresting sermons got in the way but we went to worship and loved Sunday school. The children's programs were wonderful. We grew."
As in this example, the sermon or liturgy is not always the central element of the religious experience. For some, a Sunday school class, mission group, or faith-sharing experience is more meaningful. The common element in all meaningful corporate religious experience for our sample was the opportunity to relate life concerns to symbols of religious value. This might be accomplished by the pastor in a sermon, by intercessions for the world and signs of contemporary life being present at the celebration of communion, by informal talk about everyday concerns before a Bible study, or by simply working together in an environment in which religious values were embodied.
We asked people to evaluate what impact involvement in the congregation had on their lives. This was a difficult question for those who had always been involved with a church because they had no experience of themselves apart from that involvement. Others could not make much of the question, and a few had had negative experiences. One person said simply, "[It] has little effect on my life; it is not relevant to my life." However, many people saw

important positive influences on their lives as a result of church involvement:

"Involvement in our church has helped instill a feeling of confidence and self-worth that was crushed as a result of my divorce."

"I feel that this congregation is a part of my family and because of that I have a closeness . . . If I had to leave, it would be like leaving home again."

"It has brought me closer to Christ."

"Church involvement has enriched our marriage."

"Since coming here I believe in a God I can like, maybe even love—not one to solely *fear*. I think this conversion makes me more comfortable with myself and my life."

"Now less involved in church activities. . . . The congregation has given me self-confidence—a place to seek advice and friendship."

"From studying St. Luke I find in myself a need to be of service to others and not a 'Sunday Catholic.' "

"My work with people of low income has made me more aware of community."

"My involvement has kept my faith strong, morals high, and character solid."

"My 'family,' as a single, is this parish."

"[It] is helping me to raise my children."

"[It] has helped my spiritual life grow stronger."

"[It] helped me accept people for who they are. . . ."

A maturing relationship. Several respondents in their thirties indicated that their relationship with the church had changed over the years from the dependence of childhood, the rejection of adolescence, or the intense activity of the twenties. Some people felt pulled away from church activities by family responsibilities, and others reported being disappointed or burned-out by their experience with the church. At best, however, experience with a good congregation and age seemed to bring a balance in which individuals could choose to make some contributions to the corporate life and draw from it some sustenance for the spiritual journey, as the following examples illustrate:

"My involvement has had a direct impact on my faith life; it has really deepened. The people have become friends; people I socialize with as well as pray with, do committee work with. I look at the church much differently than before—before, it was a set of rules, a structure telling me what to do, when and how to do it. Now I see church as people directing and effecting their own spiritual lives *with* the priests or religious, *not them telling me*. It's a togetherness now."

"My involvement now is more relaxed and less controlling of what happens. I do what is asked and volunteer for things, but I don't feel I have to be in on everything. . . . My life, I feel, is better, more relaxed and more able to meet problems that I may have to face.

"I am not overinvolved with the church, but I still teach because I enjoy it. I periodically volunteer for other things but nothing long-term. And I try not to be involved in everything. . . . I find myself listening more carefully to the sermons because they were mean-ingful to my life and geared toward a more sophisticated, educated person than were the sermons of the parish I grew up in. The ser-mons are people-oriented, less family-oriented. Because of this I feel I have made more of an attempt to be tolerant and Christian to-ward others. Maybe it's age also. But I feel my new relationship with the church has opened up a new relationship with God. This has helped me to realize my own limitations as a human being and I am not afraid to experiment with this relationship with God in or-der to grow."

"My involvement has steadily increased to a plateau which has and probably will prevail as it's the maximum I can handle with ef-fectiveness and personal satisfaction. My sense of spirituality contin-ues to mature both because of age and because I am here to re-ceive the nurturing which comes with worship, learning in study, and the example and fellowship of other fine Christian friends. I find it to be true for me that, for faith to grow, one must be a part of Christian community."

Age of return. The claim that young adults will "come back when they're thirty" was the original impetus for our study of if, when, how, and why people come back to the church, and what helps that process. The study indicates that if unchurched young adults affiliate with a congregation, they are likely to do so *before* age thirty. Other research also supports our finding of a median *age of return* around twenty-six or twenty-seven, with a range from about age twenty-one to thirty-four.

Thus while some adults in their twenties are in the process of returning to congregational participation, others in their early twen-ties are in the process of dropping out of active participation. That both these events are going on simultaneously, and an average dropout age of eighteen, account for the overall lower attendance rate in the twenties. The implication for congregational leaders is that they must respond to people in their twenties seeking the church even as they are ministering in other ways to those whose journey takes them away from participation in the congregation.

When it was assumed that people came back in their thirties, one hypothesis advanced was that seeking the church was part of the *"age thirty transition,* the period of reevaluation between twenty-eight and thirty-three described by Levinson and popularized by Gail Sheehy. A second hypothesis was that affiliation with a congregation might be part of the "rooting and extending" or "building of a second adult life structure" described by Levinson. In our interviews we have seen a few specific examples of each of these movements, such as the successful woman examining her life at thirty who said, "I had a good job but something was missing. . . ." Or the woman who at thirty-four said, "I was putting my life together after a divorce and it was a way of being part of a community. . . ." However, the evidence is that the majority of returnees and seekers affiliate with congregations in their twenties, in the course of building a first adult life structure. A third hypothesis, that seeking the church is related to a "crisis of limits" experienced in the thirties, is similarly rejected because the age of return falls during the optimistic twenties, before many of life's limitations become apparent.

It is said that in building a first adult life structure in their twenties, people are often controlled by images of adult life formed in childhood and by strong opinions about how life *should* be lived. We saw some evidence of this in reasons people gave for seeking the church in their twenties. Only a few people, and those often nonattenders, expressed a conscious motivation of guilt, duty, or the expectation that "I ought to go." However, many others indicated that churchgoing was a normal, expected part of adult life, especially adult family life, whose responsibilities they would assume when they were ready. If the "shoulds" dominate in the twenties as Sheehey claims, they don't make these people critical of those who don't attend church. In fact, several respondents in their twenties quite pointedly said that religion *should* be a private matter. However, the combination of opinions, hopes, and energy that make those starting adult life determined that they will not repeat the mistakes of an older generation also tend to make them more critical of the churches and older people in the churches when they do not do things "right."

Transitions. A second set of hypotheses explored by our study was based on the assumption that people seek the church and its services during life crises, passages, or transition points. It has been suggested that churches minister best in crisis and rites of passage and that programs related to life transitions draw people into con-

gregational life. We found only a few people who had been unchurched who sought help from the church or a minister at a point
of crisis. As indicated in Chapter II, influential life transitions generally precede church reentry by several months or years rather than
being the immediate or direct cause for joining a congregation.

Marriage was an event that led to church involvement for many
persons who started to date and then married a churchgoer. But
the church's preparation for marriage was seldom experienced in a
strong, positive manner, and the occasion of the marriage itself was
not cited as a point of reentry into congregational life. Similarly,
some previously unchurched parents contacted the church to have
a new child baptized, but the birth of a child was seldom cited as a
time of return to congregational participation. In fact, people often
said that their participation had decreased for two years or so after
the birth of a child because of the demands and difficulties of caring for an infant.

Given a list of life events, our sample rated the birth of a child
as the most significant change in their lives, and marriage as the
next most significant event. Although most churches have rites related to these events, we noted few specific ministries related to
other transitions rated as highly significant: change of job, major religious experience, period of depression, and change in relationship
to parents. Similarly, we found few examples of specific ministries
carried out in connection with those events most frequently reported by this sample: moving to a new home, change of job,
added volunteer service activities, and period of depression.

Part of what limits the churches in responding specifically to
transitions in individual lives is that so many people are going
through so many different transitions. One pastor cannot respond to
each person nor be expert in dealing with every issue. Few congregations are large enough to have special groups for every transition.
Given these limitations, we have seen some creative ministries at
transition points using lay leadership and external resources. In one
congregation a guild of young mothers visits parents when a child
is born, provides a support group for mothers, and manages the
church nursery. In another congregation lay persons conduct periodic spiritual journey retreats with groups of parents whose children are going to be baptized. One Roman Catholic diocese provides a training program for leaders of a citywide program for
divorced Catholics, a program which has proved most important in
the two-year adjustment period following divorce. No one parish
has many people needing this particular ministry, and turnover in
the group is high, but the citywide program with training for new
leaders seems effective. Congregations also seem to benefit from

other local, regional, or national programs reflected on the congregational level by small groups with a particular interest, such as Cursillo, Marriage Encounter, and Alcoholics Anonymous.

In some cases congregations offered short-term programs designed to respond to life events of this age-group, for example, offering a series on parenting. For the most part, these programs did not draw people from outside the congregation, and were most successful within the congregation when offered in the context of an existing program, such as an adult education forum. Congregations do help their members with life transitions but do so through their ongoing activities of worship, work, study, and fellowship. Members receive support by being able to raise their own life issues, often indirectly, in a climate of acceptance and in the presence of a religious meaning system. For example, in the age-grouped adult Sunday school class, parents may discuss their experiences raising children at the same time as they discuss some Biblical text not directly related. As they do so, the life issues are put in a new context.

An ongoing adult class can form a powerful support system, as do many small groups within the life of congregations. Not everyone, however, wishes to be part of a small group. We visited many congregations with active small groups, but we saw no instance in which attempts to organize the whole congregation into small groups (usually geographically) had been successful for over a year.

Developmental issues. We approached the interviews having in mind some of the work in ego development and faith development by such people as Erikson and Fowler. Although no attempt was made to identify the stage of each respondent, the overall weight of the evidence suggests that those seeking the church are working primarily on the life issue of *intimacy* as defined by Erikson. They often come because of their spouse or close friend. The concerns they talk about are family and friends; they value fellowship and warmth. Even the primary religious concern seems to be to feel close to God. The emphasis of many on belonging, small-group sharing, and church-related social activities further suggests that religious issues are being worked on through issues of intimacy— learning to be close to others and to share the self with others. Of course, there is some overlap with other life issues. We saw some people struggling with identity issues, and some parents beginning to work with issues of generativity.

We noted in this sample the overwhelming emphasis on belonging, the importance of the minister and other persons, and the relative absence of any talk of doctrine or intellectual struggle with the content of faith. These observations suggest that a large percentage of our respondents might be characterized by Fowler's stage three or synthetic-conventional faith (see Chapter II), the stage in which the world is understood primarily in interpersonal terms; authority figures are respected if they look the part and prove personally trustworthy. But most of those whom we interviewed have chosen their own reference groups and authorities; many changed denominations and most moved to new communities and exhibited other indications of the self-aware stage that Sharon Parks describes. However, for the majority it would be incorrect to characterize their seeking the church as the result of an intellectual search for truth and meaning. Their search could be better characterized as a diffuse seeking for friends, for a community of shared value, for support with life tasks, and a personalized but structured relationship with ultimate reality.

The cost and value of personal commitment is another life issue that gets played out in individual relationships with the congregation. For some, it is possible to stay in relationship with the congregation only so long as there is considerable freedom to come and go. It is valued that "I wasn't pushed." Then, some discover the congregation is an arena where they can commit energy because they want to, and discover there warm relationships, personal recognition, and an affirmation of their gifts. Later, many discover, as in marriage, that commitment can be confining and the relationship is not perfect.

This issue of the cost and value of commitment often gets played out around the age thirty transition, when there is also, according to Roger Gould, a renewed tendency to blame parents or spouse for one's problems. The early thirties was the age at which we most often heard about burnout, disillusionment, and reevaluation of one's activity level in the congregation. From the congregation's perspective, pastors said issues of commitment were raised for them and for older congregational members when a formerly active person in this age-group suddenly left the congregation.

We talked with several people in their late thirties who had experienced some burnout, had reevaluated their participation, and were now happy being part of a congregation without as much involvement in activities. We expect that many who experience burnout at that point leave congregational participation altogether. It seems appropriate at times for people to reduce their level of involvement with activities in the church, especially as their family and community responsibilities increase. The study suggests that congregations might help people with this transition in activity level as they move into their thirties or before burnout occurs. Also, the issues of commitment and disillusionment are appropriate raw materials for spiritual growth.

Historical change. When we first began our studies it was still being argued that the generation that came of age in the sixties was unique, had been permanently alienated from traditional, organized, Western religion, and would not return at all to church life. With the passage of time, most have returned, and the older baby-boomers are now comfortably moving into their forties.

We talked with some veterans of Vietnam, and others whose lives had been touched by the events of the sixties, but it is very difficult to detect the broad impact of historical events on the microscale of these ordinary lives. People did enjoy talking about the changes that had occurred, leading us to a new hypothesis that discovering one's own life in the fabric of contemporary history is a particular interest of young adults.

I don't want to say that everyone is coming back to church. We know from other studies that those who have chosen non-traditional lifestyles, and many of the trend-setters such as the media elite, are among those least likely to be found in churches. There do not appear to be any changes ordinary congregations might undertake to attract those persons who choose to remain unchurched.

Overall, George Gallup's figures for the church attendance rate have held roughly steady for some time. While below the unusually high level of the Eisenhower years, the general level of church participation is similar to what it was in 1940. The consistency in the churchgoing rate is particularly interesting in light of a replicated study of American child-rearing goals: in 1924, 69 percent of mothers ranked "loyalty to the church" as an important value to instill; in 1978, only 22 percent chose this goal, while 76 percent endorsed "independence or the ability of the child to think and act for himself or herself." This study and many others indicate a broad and gradual shift in values, but the claims that the new generation represents a radical break with the past have in every instance proved false.

We find young adults desirous of less rigid authoritarian structures, more participation in decisions, and a less formal public style, but these goals are not the preserve of one generation. In predominantly black congregations the younger adults we interviewed said that having a well-educated pastor was more important to them than to older adults. We assume that this reflects a higher level of education among younger African-Americans—another result of historical change.

General survey data comparing the chief concerns of young

adults today with those of young adults ten years ago reveals great differences, but we find a similarity in the concerns expressed by other adults today. As I write, interrelated concerns of success, career, economics, and the environment top the young adult agenda, but that can change rapidly with historical events.

Finally, considering the participation of churches in historical change, we cannot say that personal involvement in issues of peace and social justice is widespread. Most young adults are wrapped up in the immediate concerns of their own lives and those of their families. Some are concerned with social issues, and where we saw this expressed through the church it was significantly not through politics, policy involvement, or even social action committees, but through specific service projects in which individuals were involved. A minority are engaged in direct voluntary service to the poor, mentally ill, hungry, and sick, but these endeavors are supported by a larger number. The tendency to deal with social concerns by direct service to persons rather than by addressing issues is consistent with the predominant style of dealing with the world in interpersonal terms noted above.

A social faith. Carl Jung described the first part of life as outwardly expansive; the inward, individuative journey begins at midlife. We expected people in their twenties and thirties generally to be oriented outward. The people we talked to were very actively engaged in the world around them, and their religious life consisted more in doing than in being, meditating, or praying. We did not interview other age-groups, so perhaps this is generally true of Americans.

It does seem that the congregation as a voluntary extended family, a *fellowship* to which one belongs, may be an especially American phenomenon, accounting for the high church attendance rate in the United States. Fellowship and worship appear to be two equal parts of the congregational experience. Through worship, congregations renew people by helping them acknowledge their dependence, a process described by Bruce Reed in *The Dynamics of Religion.* Individuals say:

"The week wouldn't be right without it."

"I go to be refreshed."

"It feeds me."

People come to church for the worship, the Bible classes, the mission groups, the places where *religion* happens for them. But they also come for the fellowship, that religious experience of being together with others in a group attempting to embody and foreshadow a perfect community. Although the congregation often lapses into clannishness and the self-satisfaction of an in-group, it also challenges people by the contrast between the embodied vision of the Commonwealth of God and the competitive, broken community that members experience during the week.

In the congregations that had many newcomers and seemed "alive," there was intentional interaction between the congregation and the surrounding community. Activities at which interchange occurred included clambakes, block parties, community association meetings, seminars, community mental health projects; congregational leaders had an active presence in the daily life and work of the community. In such interactions the congregation's vision of community is shared with others and at the same time tested by everyday life. This connecting of the transcendent vision and the everyday reality is similar to what people most value when they come for their religion on Saturday or Sunday morning.

CHAPTER IV

Ministry with Young Adults

Given what we know about young adults from theory and research data, how does a congregation begin developing a young adult ministry? First, by identifying more specifically who within the wide possible age span is the intended focus for ministry. As noted in Chapter I, the challenge for ministry may be clearly provided by the demographics of the surrounding community. However, as a consultant, I have frequently found congregational groups trying to develop young adult ministry while holding vastly divergent mental pictures of the people they intended to address. It is that confusion of focus which first led us to use the catagories of explorers, pioneers, and householders in an attempt to provide a tighter focus for ministry. In this chapter we take a look at some of the practical aspects of ministry with each of these groups, beginning with the preparatory stage of youth ministry. The chapter closes with some helps for planning and getting started in young adult ministry.

Youth—Prelude to Young Adulthood

Youth ministry can provide a prelude to young adult ministry, and some styles of youth ministry carry over into the early young adult period. Six major elements of the religious life of adolescents have been identified as common for the concerns of youth ministry workers and theorists:

1. A sense of belonging, human community, being part of a group that has personal significance
2. Praying, relating to God, worshipping, ritual, having religious-sensibility
3. Having a cause to live or die for

4. Morality, rules for living
5. Meaning of life, intellectual questioning
6. Developing an integrated sense of self

(J. Ann Devitt Trevelyan, Harvard Univ. Ed.D. 1978)

Almost all people we interviewed who attended church through-out high school said that their churches had youth groups. Peer groups are very important for teenagers, and even a small active youth group in the church can support youth involvement in other congregational activities. Good youth groups encourage study, service, prayer, and discussion of life issues, besides offering fun and peer support. But the youth group is only a part of youth ministry. Even the best youth groups often involve only one third to two-thirds of the young people of a congregation in worship and inter-generational activities. Young people with little experience of being a part of the whole congregation are most likely to stop participating in the church when their involvement with the peer group ends.

Good youth ministry in a congregation takes time. Some leaders say one should start with community-building experiences in the sixth grade in order to develop a high school youth group. Good Sunday or Sabbath school experiences build toward a good youth ministry. Congregations that welcome children do a better job with youth ministry.

Good sustained youth ministry requires the commitment of the congregation's senior pastor. The pastor need not necessarily be an expert in youth ministry or even "be good with youth," but must, however, publicly affirm that young people are integral to the congregation, with as much claim as anyone else to pastoral care, recognition, and support. The pastor shows support in congregational announcements, has personal contacts with young people, advocates youth concerns with the congregation's governing board, and both recruits and supports youth advisors.

Larger congregations sometimes hire a staff person with special skills in youth ministry. This approach is often necessary and useful, but may have its problems. Youth ministry can become a "ghetto," isolating young people from contact with the pastor and others. Staff people for youth ministry are often young and hired on short-term contracts. This can harm the continuity of ministry with young people. In one congregation with few young adults, a woman observed, "We lost contact with that whole generation when we hired a seminarian to look after the youth group."

Lay people are essential to youth ministry. One study of congregations with good youth ministries found an average of one to three adults working with youth for every ten young people active in the youth group. Not all such adults were youth group advisors. Some led other activities, including Sunday school, Bible study, acolytes, choirs, or musical and dramatic groups for youth. Other adults may be involved occasionally in special projects, trips, or retreats. The involvement of many adults and support from the pastor help prevent youth leader burnout. The main requirements for lay people involved with youth are that they care about young people, take them seriously and spend time with them, and are themselves persons of faith. Youth rate the quality of their relationships with adult advisors as far more important than any particular program.

Small congregations, where clergy may change often, need committed lay leaders to maintain the leadership continuity that youth need. Although the church's having a small number of young people may make forming a peer group difficult, clergy and laity can get to know young people more personally. Occasional activities and trips may include a wide range of ages and create the context in which young people can get to know adult Christians in a new way.

The involvement of youth is supported by their being visible and receiving a positive response from the congregation. Young people may be given a role in worship as lectors, ushers, or greeters—some congregations assign these tasks by families. Visibility of youth in worship may be increased by a Youth Sunday, when young people are responsible for the congregation's worship. Youth choirs give young people an opportunity to serve and are generally well received. The support of the pastor and the involvement of many adults in these activities further encourage a positive response from the congregation.

Intergenerational activities allow youth and adults to get to know one another. They include work projects, service projects for others, softball games, picnics, and parish retreats. Although some congregations make a point of including youth on church boards and committees, this practice can be counterproductive if young people do not feel they can participate effectively. It is more important to have occasional or informal ways that youth can voice concerns.

Good youth ministry does not necessarily lead to good young adult ministry. Many congregations involve people through high school but report that the young people disappear at age eighteen. But people with a good church experience during the high school years are more likely to return. Significant relationships formed with adults then can provide a continuing and important tie with the community of faith. Further involving youth in church life beyond the family, peer group, or congregation may help them develop the portable faith needed in young adulthood.

Transitional Young Adults

Leaving high school marks entry into the early adult transition, and graduation is the closest our culture comes to having a public rite of passage to adulthood. Some churches publicly recognize graduates in the context of worship—presenting a Bible or other gift— and acknowledge that the relationship of these individuals to the congregation will change. Some pastors counsel young men about the religious aspects of draft registration, conscientious objection, or conscientious military service. Retreats during the senior year may also help young people prepare for the changes they will be experiencing. Such retreats, or personal interviews with the pastor and lay leaders, may lay the foundation for continuing personal ministries during the early adult transition.

Most youth leaders feel that, for the health of the group and for the growth of young adults, high school graduates need to leave youth groups with appropriate celebration, weeping, and ritual. Young adults may return to assist the group as youth advisors with the guidance of an older adult. Youth and young adults can work together in large group activities, such as work projects or gatherings for prayer and praise. But, young adults, who have moved past the common experience of high school and direct parental control, have concerns different from those of youth.

People ages eighteen to twenty-five move more often than does any other group in the population, and such physical mobility, combined with a characteristic psychological mobility, makes it difficult for them to establish and maintain connection with a congregation. Although ministry with people in this age group can have very important long-term consequences for the individual, it doesn't often lead to increased church participation.

Church membership records and mailing lists are seldom designed for the transient young adult. One following the job market or preparing for a career may have no permanent residence for many years; the average church dropout who reaffiliates with a congregation generally takes eight years to do so. During this extended period, the transient young adult who left the congregation after high school may still consider the congregation "home," even though he or she doesn't attend or even live in the area—witness the number of young women who still return to be married in "their church." At high school graduation, if not sooner, the church should create a separate card or listing in order to address the young adult as an individual, rather than listing him or her as a child of parental members. For those not living locally, some congregations have a status of affiliate member, which may last until the individual asks the congregation to remove or transfer his or her name.

It often helps to have a person or group maintain a list of nonresident young adults and write them. Personal contact or news from the home community can be particularly important for young people at college or in military service, although they may never say so at the time. The congregation may be kept aware of these nonresident members through a public listing of addresses, a map showing their location, or by hearing the names read during intercessory prayers.

One pastor keeps a file of young adults on whom he calls for help with Christmas services. Other congregations have a gathering for students during the Christmas season. Where distances permit, some congregations send their pastors on annual visits to students at residential colleges. Such approaches allow congregations to show their continuing concern for young adults who are part of the fellowship but not present by reason of their vocation.

Other young adults facing similar transitional issues remain in the local community to work or attend college. Since their change of status is not so clear, some people in the congregation continue to treat them as children. In a way, these young adults need to be treated as newcomers and be personally invited to participate in adult activities and leadership according to their gifts. Many younger adults are good Sunday school teachers, advisors to acolytes or youth, or choir members. Opportunities for physical activity in work projects or sports can be especially attractive to young people just out of high school. But getting them involved in activities is not enough. Young adults want and need contact with adults with whom they can discuss their own growth and faith.

Some transitional young adults want the continuing support of a peer group in the congregation, and there are various ways to provide this. The larger congregation may have a "college and career" class as part of an adult Sunday school. Another approach is a small faith-sharing group or monthly informal gathering. One bachelor pastor in a small church invites young adults to supper once a month, and to stimulate conversation occasionally has special guests.

Transitional young adults can rely more on their own leadership than is characteristic of youth groups, but some support from the congregation or staff is necessary. Because of the transiency of this group, it is important for the pastor or other congregational leadership to respond quickly to expressed needs, rather than try to develop a large or long-range program. Very few congregations have large numbers in this age-group, and ongoing large groups for transitional young adults require a great deal of time and energy from leaders—extra staff is usually necessary.

Late adolescents are particulary open to ideology and idealism. Thus cults are a danger to some young people in this difficult transitional period. Cults express clearly and energetically how the world is and what one ought to do. Cults offer warm support and membership in a close group, preying especially on those who feel friendless. Similarly, young adults can be attracted to ideological presentations of Christianity from magnetic leaders.

The ideological mind of young adults may be expressed in intense intellectual searching and hard questions about the faith. Opportunities to express such ideas and concerns in the life of the congregation are important to young adults. Parents and other adults in the congreation should understand that questioning is not "unfaith" but a particular kind of searching faith. Young adults need the opportunity to "give their lives away" in service at home or abroad. Although many denominational and ecumenical service opportunities exist, these are not always clearly made available to young adults. Some congregations financially support young adults in voluntary service and, by informing themselves about those serving in distant places, have developed a tradition of young adult service. Close to home, if an older member invites young adults, they may become very involved in congregational service projects that require direct action, such as working in a soup kitchen. Short-term work projects can also be used to raise issues of service and vocation with young adults.

Most transitional young adults are single as they leave adolescence, but a majority will marry by the end of this period. Marriage is an opportunity to minister. We find that pastors who give special attention to premarital counseling are likely to be sought out by unchurched young adults in the community. Some pastors who are unable to make a specialty of this ministry refer a couple to premarital courses in the area, and then meet with the couple briefly. Other pastors ask the engaged couple to meet with a married couple in the congregation to discuss their expectations of marriage. Such an approach helps build a relationship with adults other than the pastor. One pastor simply asks the engaged couple to attend church together for six weeks. He says, "In that time, they will hear whatever I have to say and see what we are all about." However marriage preparation is handled, the way churches treat people at this point is an important witness about the church for the couple and young adults who attend the wedding.

Churches near a college, military base, or other facility that draws young adults from outside the area have a special ministry of welcoming the transient stranger. Specialists in institutional ministry from denominational agencies can direct those congregations in special circumstances to appropriate resources. Young adult males, in particular, may be the hardest to reach, but are most in need of ministry. In the society as a whole, transitional young adult males run the greatest risk of death by accident, homicide, or suicide; account for a large proportion of the crime; and have a high rate of unemployment. To respond to these young adults the church may be called to special ministries of outreach or advocacy.

Transitional young adults can be interesting friends and can enliven a congregation with their energy and fresh vision of the world. They don't carry the weight of experience, so generally they are open to new possibilities and responsive to current history and culture. Working on discovering their own values and place in the world, they can be open to taking the Gospel seriously in their lifestyle and vocation. Although long-term commitment may not be possible for them, they can be intensely committed to a group or project for a brief time.

Personal contact is the key to ministry with this group. They need someone to take an interest in them and listen to them. Few need long-term counseling, but respond more readily than other age-groups to brief encounters. When personal contact has been established, they may be very responsive to short-term activities, such as an intensive Bible study, a service project, or an outdoor retreat.

Adults in Their Twenties

After moving away from home, schooling, various entry-level jobs, and other transitions, young adults become somewhat more settled. They make some decisions about career, marriage, and lifestyle. These choices may not be fixed for life, but there is a greater sense of identity. They know "who I am and how I fit into the world." These young adults are making their own way in the world, doing many things for the first time, and building a new world for themselves—they are "pioneers."

One-third of people in their twenties have moved in the past year, so they are often new to the community. Among the tasks that many do on their own for the first time is to seek out the church.

Return to the church for dropouts or a new involvement with congregational life commonly occurs in this period, with a median age of return at age twenty-six or twenty-seven.

Most young adults believe in God and are not hostile to religion. However, they may have negative images of organized religion and limited contact with churchgoers. They are busy people, and churchgoing may not be a priority. People in transition tend not to seek out the church. When they are more settled, it is hard to find a new community of believers that one is comfortable with. Few young adults just walk into a church and say, "Where do I join?" Most can't say just what they are looking for. A few shop around for a church. The first moves toward a church are likely to be tentative. The time from initial contact to active involvement with a congregation can take two or more years. Congregations need to reach out to these pioneer young adults, welcome them, incorporate them into congregational life, and nurture their faith.

To consider involvement with a church at all, one must be able to find it. At the simplest level, a church may improve access with signs, newspaper ads, listings in the yellow pages, and a 24-hour telephone response at the church giving hours of service. Young adults for whom the church is unfamiliar are helped by clear and attractive signs showing service times, office hours, and where to find the office, classes, and activities. One congregation has eye-catching newspaper ads at Easter and Christmas, times when young adults may be drawn to the church. Another announces special activities in papers frequently read by single people in the community. One congregation advertises a "listening post" for alienated church members, another invites people to an open house featuring "What the Church is Like Today."

Community activities help make the church accessible for people. One large church sponsors a continuing education festival with varied classes; a small church runs a vacation Bible school for all the children of a community. Another small church sponsors a town festival; a city church offers periodic seminars of interest to young single adults; another holds concerts. Many churches offer their facilities to community groups, increasing the church's visibility and its service. Some churches sponsor professional pastoral counseling services, and a few underwrite ministries of outreach to special groups in the community, such as non-English-speaking groups, the mentally handicapped, apartment dwellers, or the homeless.

The church becomes most visible through people. Churchgoing young adults aften report that they first met the pastor in some community activity. Several rural churches hold annual fellowship dinners to which church members invite a friend. Estimates are that up to 90 percent of all new church members first come with a friend or family member.

Like others, young adults need to feel they are welcome members of the whole congregation. A greeting at the door, a personal guide to the coffee hour, and the identification of lay leaders helps. In some congregations elected leaders make announcements or have distinctive name tags to make themselves known. Several churches serve a Sunday brunch, thus creating an informal atmosphere in which people can talk after services. One congregation makes a special point of greeting the many young people who attend Christmas Eve services, another extends a community invitation during December to young adults to sing in an informal Christmas choir.

It has been said that visitors are most likely to come back if they are visited within seventy-two hours of their initial visit to a church, and that an invitation to serve in some capacity increases an individual's feeling of belonging. But young adults are often ambivalent in their approach to the church and may not be ready to commit themselves. A congregation needs to communicate interest in the person and his or her journey and gifts rather than sell a church or a job.

However young adults enter a church, what is important is what they find there. Most churches have more young adults coming through their doors than they realize, but the young adults don't stay. Congregations that design their worship and activities mainly for their members over forty seldom have many young adults. Young adults are looking for religion that relates to their lives and a sense of belonging. One says what he is looking for is "something you can apply to everyday life and friends you can count on." Another describes it as "an open, honest, friendly atmosphere conducive to spiritual growth."

For most congregations, worship is the chief expression of their religious life, which may also be expressed through Bible study, prayer groups, study, and service. Whatever other activities a church may offer, young adults will not be involved in the congregation unless it offers a religious expression related to their lives. One congregation that sponsored a large community club for young adults found that few of these young adults would participate in the church's worship because they found it "too formal, all dark suits and gray hair."

For almost all young adults, the worship in a new congregation will differ from what they know. In many places, one-half of new young members come from other denominations or lack any church background at all. Newcomers need help and instruction in local practices. Because many young adults respond to less formal worship and contemporary music, congregations may incorporate these into worship or offer alternative services. In many congregations with active young adults, young people help plan and lead worship, especially for special occasions. And one pastor serving many young adults correctly observes, "Everything we do in worship must be first-class."

Some churches have groups that help prepare sermons by reflecting on the text with the preacher, and some have sermon feedback groups. When young adults are in these groups they help the pastor understand young adult needs and issues to be addressed. Sermons are very important to young adults. If they have come to a church, they are looking for some connection between the transcendent and their own lives.

An adult Sunday school class, prayer group, or study group may also provide the corporate link with the transcendent. It is not as important to address life issues in the class content as it is to allow people to discuss their life concerns, even informally, in a religious context. One group of young adults said that the coffeepot time before a Bible study was their opportunity for meaningful conversation about their life concerns.

Socializing is important for this age-group, permitting them to have fun, make friends, and discuss serious concerns. Young adults talk with their friends about many life decisions and views of the world. As we have seen, they are working on the issue of intimacy, learning to share oneself with others. Young adults also learn to be intimate with God through their relationships. Many successful programs for this age-group offer a large-group social time, small discussion groups, and worship in which personal concerns can be offered.

Some young adults want immediate intense involvement with a small group that may become a substitute family for a while. Others need the freedom to hang back and observe without commitment. Congregations with many young adults tend to support various degrees of involvement. Physical activity as well as discussion is important. One congregation has a "Helping Hands" group through which young adults do physical tasks for members and nonmembers. Activities involving young adults may include faith-sharing groups, retreats, hiking, canoe trips, social service activities, choirs, or sports.

The chance for leadership is important. Pioneer young adults often discover that while one can be an effective adult in the world, in the church one must be a white male with twenty years of seniority in order to be even an usher. There is no congregational job

that people in their twenties cannot handle and are not already doing in some congregation. Young adults want to do a good job. To
do so they need to know what is expected, freedom to do the job,
support from peers and leaders, and freedom to fail or back out
gracefully if necessary.

It is not enough simply to involve people in activities. Frequently, young adults become involved in active leadership in a
congregation because they want opportunities for contact and spiritual growth with the pastor and committed people. Bringing young
adults into a congregation involves reaching out, welcoming, providing avenues of involvement, instructing newcomers, celebrating
membership, and encouraging participation in decision-making.
However, the congregation must also nurture further spiritual
growth and support people in their work and outreach in the
world.

Moving and a change of job are the most frequent transitions for
young adults. Work, career issues, changing work responsibilities,
unemployment, and new jobs are important concerns. One church
has a group to help people discern their vocation; another invites
leading professionals to address ethical concerns in the workplace;
another offers a support group for the unemployed.

"Pioneer" young adults are more settled than transitional: however, because of their developing careers, many are still subject to
frequent moves. They may become involved in a congregation, but
then have to move within two years. Therefore, congregations need
to allow people to become involved quickly, and need to pay attention to departures. Churches must publicly recognize and celebrate
in some way the departure of people from the congregation. When
the grief of parting is acknowledged, and good-byes are said, it is
easier for those leaving to become involved in a new congregation,
and easier for those who remain to invest themselves in other new
people who may not stay long.

Married young adults. Marriage often results in new church members. Couples inclined to churchgoing generally look for a church
in which both partners are comfortable. Because one partner has a
stronger church investment than the other, the couple goes to "his"
church or "her" church. Thus the couple brings into the congregation a nonmember who may find things strange. If this nonmember
feels welcome and comfortable, the couple is likely to stay. If the
nonmember feels the church is too demanding, religion can cause
conflict in the marriage. As a result, the couple drops church participation altogether.

Newly married couples without children still have much of the freedom of young single people, and may frequently be away from church on weekend trips. They may be most comfortable among unmarried friends. Where there are many young couples in a church, they frequently form a lively group with mutual contact outside as well as in the church. Such groups are best tagged with a name, such as "The Maranatha Class," rather than being called the "Couples Club."

Both men and women rate having a child as one of the most significant events in their lives. Having a child causes other relationships to change and new feelings to awaken in the parents. The church may be a part of this experience through pastoral care and public ritual. Many congregational members prize little bits of ritual associated with infants: parents placing a rose on the altar at infant dedication or the priest carrying the child into the midst of the congregation after a baptism.

Churches that practice infant baptism find it most helpful to the spiritual growth of parents to elicit stories and feelings from parents rather than simply to instruct them in the context of learning about baptism. Lay people in one congregation offer Saturday workshops in which parents and sponsors share their own spiritual journeys and hopes for their children. Parents may be similarly involved in reflection and learning in churches that admit young children to communion. Several churches regard parents as the chief Christian educators of young children and offer programs to help parents with this task.

Ongoing and sensitive contact with new parents is also important because the birth of a child can become for some an occasion of dropping out of active church involvement. Few parents are really prepared for the overwhelming disruption that caring for an infant can cause. Especially when both parents work, no time and energy may be left for anything else.

Congregations with many young families provide child care for all activities. In one such congregation, an infant can be in the nursery from 8 a.m. until noon on Sunday. This allows the parents to worship and take part in the other activities. With the rise of professional day-care centers, parents are applying stiffer standards to church child care, and the old room under the basement steps is no longer acceptable.

Congregations ministering to young families usually provide child care and welcome children in worship. Some parents highly value having their children with them. Others find that they cannot themselves worship while they are responsible for young children. The congregations that do best with young families allow parents to either bring their children to church or to place them in child care.

Childen in worship may disturb some members of the congregation. To deal with this problem most churches have a family service and another service at which children generally are not present. Sunday school arrangements that overlap the worship hour and have children come for part of the service are popular, as are schedules with Sunday school and adult education before or after worship.

Most young parents want religious instruction for their children. As public preschool programs have become popular, there is a growing expectation that some formal Christian education program, instead of just child care, will begin with three- and four-year-olds. Where there is a really excellent program for children, the children's desire to participate may bring parents to church. However, few parents continue to attend church just for the sake of the children. The lack of good religious education for children will probably keep young parents away from a congregation, but its presence is no guarantee of their continued participation unless they find something for themselves as well.

Like other young adults, young parents seek a vital religious life that speaks to their concerns and needs for participation in a community. The family service allows them to bring the family, their chief concern, into the worship life of the community. Like their single peers, young parents need to socialize and discuss life issues. They need congregational contexts in which to discuss family concerns. Almost any prayer, study, or work group in which there are many other young parents can meet their need. Such groups may address family concerns from time to time, using a film series, for example. But programs on the concerns of parents usually don't draw in many outsiders unless they are widely advertised and offered to the community at large at a time other than Sunday morning.

Single young adults. Much of the literature on young adult ministry is exclusively about single young adults; the terms *young adult* and *single* are interchangeable for many people. However, the concern for single people goes well beyond those in the young adult years. Over 50 percent of all single adults are over thirty, and 25 percent are over sixty-five. A third of the adult population is single. Concern for ministry with single people has increased as a growing number of single people have made it known that they felt neglected by heavily family-centered churches. Many churches still discriminate unwittingly against single people. For example, pastors may use only sermon examples drawn from family life, family night dinners are announced, family men are regarded as better leaders, and so on. Single people can help the church avoid such discrimination by raising the issue and by nominating single people for boards and committees.

While "young adult" groups don't work well, many congregations have singles groups because common elements of the single life span age-barriers. However, such groups seldom include the transitional young adults age eighteen to twenty-five who often see themselves as "not-yet-married." An ongoing singles group may be possible only in large, multiple-staff churches. Smaller churches, however, may have events chiefly involving single people. Singles in the congregation may want to organize an occasional seminar, Sunday brunch, trip, or activity away from the church. Single people always need to be involved in the planning to meet their needs. They may also be encouraged to take the lead in organizing events for the whole congregation, such as square dances and caroling parties.

Single leaders from one congregation suggest a congregation can do the following to involve singles: use singles as readers, assistant ministers, planners of worship, and helpers at various functions; sponsor seminars with topics of concern to single people; build a support system for them; involve singles in special parish ministries, such as visiting the elderly, teaching Christian education, leading youth activities, parish plays, and outings; invite singles to be a part of parish committees; address their concerns from the pulpit and select prayers appropriate for singles.

Ministry with single young adults can feel particularly threatening to a congregation because it may raise sexuality issues that the congregation is uncomfortable dealing with. How one relates to others as a sexual person is a particular concern of many single people. They, like others, need to bring their life concerns into the religious context. A congregation that will not address sexuality, or that treats all people as asexual in the religious context, probably will not have many single young adults. On the other hand, a congregation can be enriched by taking seriously this dimension of life. Single people have many gifts and can bring a new understanding of the congregation as a community of friends.

Adults in Their Thirties

If people in their twenties are often impatient with the way the world is run, people in their thirties are likely to be responsible for the day-to-day operation of some small part of the world. They are more likely to be employed, be engaged in volunteer activities, and have children at home than any other age-group. Almost all live on their own or in families for which they are responsible. They are householders, a stage of life some Eastern religions identify between life as a "student" and "the forest journey" (See Chapter II).

The thirtieth birthday looms as a marker for many people in their late twenties. In retrospect, people often find they experienced a significant transition in their lives between the ages of twenty-eight and thirty-three. It is a common period for divorce and major career changes. It is still true that few women have a first child after age thirty, and a majority have completed childbearing by that age. Levinson sees the *age 30 transition* as a period in which stresses from the first adult life structure are adjusted, some personal limitations are realized, and a more permanent, second adult-life structure is created.

We found many young adults who had become active in congregational life reevaluating their involvement in this age thirty transition. For two reasons some experienced church burnout. First, some became disillusioned because their active church involvements led them to discover the limitations of congregational life and the human failings of the church's leaders. Second, some became overcommitted to church activities and found that with increased responsibilities at home and at work they had to reduce church activities. In some congregations, there seemed to be no way to do this gracefully.

People in their thirties are generally very willing to assume responsibility at work and in the community. They move less frequently than do people in their twenties and have more community involvements. They are active volunteers and good candidates for lay leadership in the church. They allocate their time among various responsibilities, and whereas younger adults are apt to become intensely involved in a short-term project, those who are older are more likely to commit themselves to a once-a-month engagement for years. These willing volunteers can become overcommitted. One church avoids this by not allowing any member to assume more than two responsibilities at once in the congregation.

Women, who once served as the mainstays of church volunteer work, are now much more likely to be employed, especially as their children reach school age. A congregation's expectation that all women should volunteer can induce guilt or hostility in these women with very busy lives. Churches need to adjust their activities to the reality of working women. For example, one congregation found that young families better supported a Wednesday night supper and program when various groups prepared the meal than when participants were asked to bring a covered dish.

Family life is the chief concern of most people in their thirties.

Forms of family life are changing. There are many more single-parent families and blended families now, but the commitment to family life remains strong. A major motivation for congregational involvement in this group is the expectation that the church will support family life.

People in their thirties may have both teenagers and toddlers. They value activities families can do together and worship involving children. This is the group most supportive of family night suppers, family camping retreats, Sunday school picnics, and intergenerational activities of all kinds. They like children's sermons and special services with a family atmosphere such as Christmas pageants, Halloween services, the dedication of children on Mother's Day, outdoor celebrations, and the Blessing of Pets on the Feast of St. Francis. They support children's choirs, acolytes, Scouts, Sunday schools, and youth groups.

Single parents and parents who come to church single generally appreciate those intergenerational activities that support family life so long as language and activities oriented to couples are avoided. When parents need to be involved in activities for children, sensitive congregations avoid exclusive references to mothers or fathers, for example, not planning father/son or mother/daughter activities.

Divorce between people in the congregation is difficult to deal with. Married couples often feel threatened by the divorce of others, and people who are divorcing often feel alienated from the church. Individual pastoral care is always appropriate, but special groups for divorced people are generally most helpful only during a two-year transition after the divorce. Such support groups are often effectively offered areawide rather than by a single congregation. The individual congregation that has shown it accepts single and divorced people can minister most effectively to people going through divorce.

People without children are a minority among householders. Many enjoy and participate in family-oriented intergenerational activities, and some eagerly welcome the opportunity to be with children, such as in teaching Sunday school. However, they also seek opportunities for adult study, worship, and activities not involving children or a discussion of children. Those without children may be particularly able to help the church look beyond care of its own to address service to others, community concerns, and larger issues.

Some shift in social action concerns occurs during the young adult years. There may be a change from an ideological stance toward a concern for concrete local action. A minority of church people are involved in social issues, such as hunger, peace, and justice. Those we see effectively involved through the church are more likely to be a part of direct service groups than issue study groups. People in their thirties are helpful in organizing local service projects because of their sense of responsibility and community involvements. Many in this group are involved in community concerns beyond the church, and congregations can acknowledge and support these individual ministries without drawing people into church-related activities.

Serious illness can strike at any age, and among young adults has a heightened impact because it feels untimely. In one congregation, when a thirty-year-old was discovered to have cancer, the whole congregation had to work through the issue of why this happened and how they could respond to a young individual who had "contracted death." Immediate physical help from members of the congregation may be appropriate when a parent with family responsibilities or a single person separated from extended family is affected. As young adults move into their thirties, their chances of being affected by the illness of a parent or child increase. Young parents with a seriously ill child often need special support. Hospital chaplains report that during times of severe crisis young adults often regress to religious forms from an earlier period of their lives.

For those who experience the illness or death of a parent living some distance away, the attention of the congregation to this event—visiting the family or holding a memorial service—can be very important. In our interviews one man said that he was moved to discover that his congregation had sent flowers to his mother's funeral in another state; a Catholic woman said she was drawn closer to the church after the priest had demonstrated his caring by attending her father's Protestant funeral. Another person said that a visit by the pastor on the anniversary of his father's death was very helpful. People in their thirties often experience some continuing tension with their parents, and it may be helpful to address directly these concerns in a study group.

Changes in the patterns of church participation may occur for people in their late thirties. Parents with teenage children become more concerned with youth activities, and those who live far from the church may look for a church closer to home if they drive their children to many activities. Some parents drop out of church involvement when their children leave home. As people begin to work on midlife issues, they may want to reduce their involvement in activities and groups while increasing interest in prayer and spiritual growth. Activity and responsibility characterize the spirituality of householders, while after midlife the interior journey may become more important.

Summary

Between age eighteen and the end of the thirties people move from adolescence to midlife. In these years individuals focus energy on the outward journey, creating a place for themselves in the world as adults. Erikson identifies their development issues as identity, intimacy, and generativity. These three issues correspond with the concerns of subgroups we label explorers, pioneers, and householders.

Transitional young adults, generally between ages eighteen and twenty-five, are the most mobile—in transition between school and work and moving from life with parents to life on their own. These explorers are open to experiments, to ideology, and to intense involvements. They are the least likely to be regular churchgoers. Keys to ministry with these explorers include the following:

—Keep in personal contact; provide mentors and discipling.
—Focus on short-term events: retreats, work projects, intensive Bible study.
—Offer opportunities for voluntary service.
—Be open to questions in classes or informal "raps."
—Get physical: sports, service, wilderness adventures.
—Use popular culture: music, films, etc.
—Respond to changing needs for peer groups, individual action, intergenerational contact.

Adults in their twenties are most likely to seek new congregational involvement. Churches need to respond to them by reaching out to, welcoming, and incorporating these new adults who have new ideas and different lifestyles. These pioneer adults, whether single or married, need congregational entry points, friends, and opportunities to socialize.

Householders, adults in their thirties, are more settled, with greater work, home, and community responsibilities. They want to bring these concerns into church life. Mostly parents, they like family church activities. Education for children and child care during activities and meetings help their involvement. They need concrete opportunities for service and spiritual growth. Support groups and ritual help with transitions and hard realities—limitations, family conflicts, illness, death and other loss.

Age-specific programs are a small part of ministry with young adults. Congregations need to include younger adults in the community of faith and empower them for service in the world. In widely different congregations, we found young adults attracted by what they perceived as a living faith, convincingly believed and lived in relation to their world.

Planning for Young Adult Ministry

What do they want? This question often betrays little personal involvement and understanding of whoever *they* are. People beginning young adult ministry often ask this question. Because ministry must engage people, the best way to answer the question is through greater personal involvement. One woman who developed an excellent ministry with young adults said, "I didn't know anything about young adult ministry, so I just started visiting all the young adults in the congregation to get to know them."

Congregations may occasionally survey their members by a written interest inventory. More than one program planner has found that young adults are interested in many things but that such interest does not mean they will attend a program planned around that interest. For example, many young adults express interest in Bible study, but don't attend church Bible studies. Interest is more likely to be acted on if one is personally invited and involved in the planning. Therefore, interest inventories with names on the returns are more helpful than an anonymous questionnaire. For purposes of ministry, identifying five people who share a common concern is far more valuable than knowing that 20 percent of the group is "interested."

Some congregations have tried to start a young adult ministry with a needs assessment of young adults in the community. Often this has not resulted in any action. Young adults have many needs, and the stated needs are usually beyond the capacity of the congregation to address. Unfortunately, when young adults are asked directly about their needs, they become hopeful that something will be done. When little happens, disillusionment with the church increases. An alternative approach is to ask knowledgeable community people about young adult needs. This approach informs the congregation about what is already being done and helps develop contacts with others working with young adults in the community.

A needs assessment or consultation with community experts is most appropriate for congregations seeking to meet human needs other than just religious needs. Such congregations have developed programs to serve special needs, such as drop-in medical clinics, counseling centers, social clubs, ESOL (English for Speakers of Other Languages), soup kitchens, and day-care centers.

Religious needs generally don't show up on needs assessments, although congregations are best prepared to respond to these needs. Many young adults either don't feel a religious need, or are inarticulate about it. As noted in Chapter III, the Gallup organization found that nearly half of the unchurched who returned to active church participation responded "don't know" or gave no answer when asked why they had returned to church. The desire for religion we have identified in young adults is seldom stated directly, but religion is what people seem to be looking for. The business of the church may be, as one pastor put it, "to deal with real needs, not felt needs."

When the Dayton Young Adult Study asked those eighteen to twenty-nine years old the ways they thought organized religion was failing to do the job it should, they mentioned the following:

—fails to meet the needs of people.
—apathetic, uninspired.
—too materialistic, too preoccupied with money.
—out-of-date, out of touch with reality.
—not reaching young people.
—too many hypocrites.
—too smug.
—not true faith.
—not digging into the real problems facing humankind.

It's a hard list to respond to, but asking in general what's wrong may not be very helpful. The Gallup Poll has shown that churched and unchurched people share many of the same criticisms of organized religion. Although many young adults have negative feelings about organized religion, it seems that more don't participate simply because they don't have friends who attend or any strong desire to go to church.

The congregation may not be able to make the unchurched young adult attend, but it can make attending easier for those who seek the church. Those who have recently joined the church can tell the congregation about what helps and hinders the process. The following four questions are ones that we have used to good effect:

1. What helped involvement? (What first attracted you to this congregation? What helped your transition into this particular congregation?)
2. What was negative? (What almost stopped you from involvement in this congregation? What are the problems for you in this congregation? What turns you off?)

3. What do you like now? (What holds you here? Where are the places your needs are met? What draws you into deeper involvement?)
4. What advice do you have for this congregation?

Asking young adults their advice is a first step; involving them in planning and decision making is the next.

As young adults begin to enter a congregation, there will be some tension between old people and new people. The situation is somewhat similar to that of a rural congregation which finds itself ministering to people from a new suburb. There is both pleasure at the sight of new members and some conflict of cultures. The tensions can be creative if the leadership recognizes that they are there and is committed to building a congregation inclusive of new and old.

A mistake larger congregations often make is to hire an associate to work with young adults without making an overall attempt to incorporate young adults into the congregation. If the new associate is at all successful in attracting young adults, some incident of conflict inevitably develops between young and old. All too often, the blame is laid on the associate, who eventually resigns.

The inclusion of new people inevitably brings change as they bring new needs and different styles. Young adults will not stay in a congregation if control is vested in an old guard that does not value the gifts and contributions of the new. Today's young adults expect to participate in decisions affecting them, and if they have any influence, change will occur.

All parish leaders have experienced resistance to innovation in the church. "We can't do that because the older members would object" is often heard, but such resistance relates more to the loss of the familiar than to the presence of the new. There is less resistance if activities responsive to young adult needs are added, than if existing programs are changed. For example, innovations in worship first made outside the context of the existing worship services bring greater acceptance. Pastors who have successfully incorporated young adults into older congregations say that one key is to make sure older members feel supported and not neglected as change comes about.

Incorporating young adults means incorporating diversity—the new people are different from the old and young adults themselves are diverse. One way to permit the new to grow up alongside the old is to help new people develop informal groups and occasional activities that do not require the permission of existing parish leadership. For example, young adults can be encouraged to begin a faith-sharing group or plan a ski weekend without making it an official part of the congregation's program. One governing board recognized that its deliberate way of making decisions often slowed action on matters that it did not need to decide. An "Issues Fair" was held. Parish members wrote issues they were concerned about on signs, then milled around, talking with people who had similar interests. Several projects involving young and old developed from the fair. A congregation can nurture many diverse people through groups and activities that are announced but not directly controlled by the congregation.

A church can also nurture diverse needs by using outside resources. Representatives in the congregation can help people participate in outside programs, such as a divorce support group or a spiritual renewal movement. Various congregations invite outsiders to conduct a weekend of renewal, a family education course, a preaching mission, a workshop on the single life, or other such activities. Many educators feel the best education is developed locally out of the life issues of the participants. But some congregations find that professionally produced programs and films can provide the content around which people can raise their own issues. Using such resources is another way the congregation can address diverse needs on an occasional basis without becoming specialists in a multitude of subjects.

Whether planning for a specific program or for the general inclusion of young adults in the congregation, involving young adults is essential in the planning process. In every aspect of young adult ministry a team approach has proved most useful. Here, a team means a semiformal group working together on a particular task in which the members of the group may change while the task continues. Such teams in young adult ministry overcome the problem of a lack of continuity resulting from the high mobility of young adults. These teams allow people to become involved quickly while assuming responsibility at their own pace. Young adult ministry teams must attend to individual needs and group process, thus meeting young adult needs for intimacy as well as working on a task. When older adult members are also on the team, the emphasis on relationships helps the group build an inclusive community. Team members can demonstrate for the congregation good relationships between generations. The team approach also has the benefit of including views from a variety of young adults, rather than relying on the perspective of one or two, who may not be typical.

Ministry planning must be responsive to local schedules and values. All churches tend to absorb and reflect incidental styles and values of the communities they serve. Thus one congregation has a clambake, a second has a bean supper, a third has a wine-and-cheese party. A country church has a 5:30 a.m. fellowship breakfast for young farmers while a city congregation has a late-night prayer group. One community of householders values the do-it-yourself ethic and likes work parties at the church, while another wants to contribute professional expertise. Congregations successful with young adults understand these differences and adapt to those styles of young adult life that are a matter of preference, not Gospel. In one place this means vegetarian dinners and sandals in church; a second, hot dogs and ball games; a third, drama groups and white wine. One church has a gospel choir, another a guitar mass. Although generalizing about young adults is difficult, many desire less formal relationships and more personal forms of religion—for example, passing the peace in worship and the public offering of private concerns for prayer.

One cannot forget personal religious growth in planning for young adult ministry. Many young adults, even the unchurched, have had some experience with small Bible study groups and may want the opportunity to continue that. About one-third of young adults report having had some intense religious experience. Pastoral listening and faith-sharing groups can help them build on that experience. Issues of vocation and Christian calling in one's work may be explored in relation to job-related concerns. Young adults may be most willing to talk about spiritual concerns in retreat settings, where they are away from daily responsibilities and have developed a group they trust.

Ministry with young adults goes beyond reaching out and assimilating new members to nurturing growth and service in the world. For each age-group discussed, congregational planners can use other criteria from their own mission statements to evaluate ministry. For example, one can ask, How are people in each age-group involved in worship, study, service, evangelism, and pastoral care? or What are the opportunities at each age for experience, affiliation, searching, and commitment in faith?

To get started in young adult ministry, your most important resources are your faith and love for people, together with the gifts of your congregation. Identify what you and your congregation have to offer. The most significant ministries are built on existing strengths and local resources. People are resources for ministry. Identify young adults and those who are working with them in your church and community. Enlist their help. Clergy serving other churches and institutional chaplains in your area may have expertise they are willing to share. Such people may also know of local resources, such as good locations to hold a retreat, film libraries, and people from whom you can learn skills. Skills in group development and simple methods of lay-led Bible study are particularly useful in this ministry. Finally, your denomination probably has staff people and materials to help you. Ask if resources are available from your denominational office of young adult or family life ministries. Because resources in this field change rapidly, I have included no listing here.

Planning for young adult ministry begins with meeting individuals and listening to their concerns. Invite them to participate in various teams to develop activities and worship. Nurture diversity; help people develop events and small groups that meet their particular interests. Support volunteers through training for tasks, limited time commitments, and continuing personal contact. Remember, PLANS mean Personal contact, Listening, Action teams, Nurture, and Support.

With transitional young adults, ministry may be done primarily through individual contact and occasional events. With adults in their twenties and older, ministry can't be done "off to the side" but involves incorporating new members into congregational life. Congregational leaders must support older members while planning for the future congregation.

Young adults are as diverse as the whole population. No magic formula will attract them. They may come to the church to be with friends or family; few come from guilt, duty, or habit. Generally they have an underlying desire for some connection between their own lives and something larger, some religious meaning. They bring varied concerns, values, needs, and gifts. The congregation is challenged to incorporate what they bring and to share with them its own life and religious tradition. What emerges from this interaction will be a new congregation. It is my hope that this new congregation will not only incorporate people but also empower them for life and service in the world.

Beyond Young Adulthood

Our studies of young adult ministry began initially with the challenge of the baby-boom generation, and it may be fitting to close with a word about this group as they begin to move beyond young adulthood. The 1980's saw a number of articles and new publications about the baby-boom generation. The oldest members of the baby-boom generation turned forty in 1986, and several national magazines responded with cover stories on the baby-boom generation. *U.S. News and World Report* dated the birth of the baby-boom as May of 1946, nine months after VJ day, when the United States recorded a record high number of births. In November of 1986, Hartford Seminary released its study documenting the fact that the church participation rate for older baby boomers had approached the national average for all adults. A number of religion editors around the country had noticed the boomers' return to religion in their own communities and were writing stories on the phenomenon.

Demographers define the baby boom generation as inclusive of those people born during the years 1946 through 1964. During those years the United States experienced record annual numbers of births, a trend fed by higher rates of family formation and conservative social trends. Thus, the baby-boom generation includes everyone between the ages of twenty-six and forty-four in 1990, about one third of the US population. However, it is common to recognize at least two distinct generational experiences within the baby-boom generation. The older baby boomers, born between 1946 and 1954, generally had some personal memory of the more stable, conservative, optimistic, but racially segregated post-war culture. They were old enough to be in school by 1960. Almost all recall the assassination of John Kennedy as an early significant historical event. They were "youth" during the sixties and all turned eighteen before the end of the Vietnam draft. When they were younger, much was written about a "generation gap" with parents, but these older, "Challenger" baby boomers are now thirty-seven to forty-four years old, themselves parents.

Their younger brothers and sisters are a numerically larger group to whom less attention has been paid. Born between 1955 and 1964, they include children from the peak birth years who have always experienced some crowding and competition for a seat on the bus, space in the lunchroom, admission to college, or a job at the factory. Coming of age in the seventies, they experienced gas lines early in their driving careers. Children during the Vietnam War, they did not experience a common consensus about American life and values and they are more likely to have lived a time with only one parent. Having experienced early a need to compete and a society in transition, and having come of age in a period of retrenchment, they tend to be more conservative than the older baby boomers. This group, described by Douglas Walrath as "Calculators," are still young adults in the early 1990s.

But what of the front of the wave, those so well described in Landon Jones' book *Great Expectations?* Writing about those older baby boomers, *U.S. News and World Report* (March 10, 1986) reported that of those age forty, 84% attended high school, 44% attended college, and 25% have at least a four-year degree. Eighty percent of the men, and 77% of the women are currently married, and 87% of the women have had at least one child. Political consultant Lee Atwater noted, " . . . Today's typical forty-year-old is socially tolerant, conservative on economic issues, and more apt to be an independent than the population at large." Dr. Carol Nadelson of the American Psychiatric Association said of them, "The forty-year-old's most common complaint is "Why haven't I got what I expected? . . . These people were told promises can be fulfilled if they worked hard. But they worked hard, and their promises weren't fulfilled."

When these older baby boomers first became young adults, they helped lead an exodus from America's churches in the sixties and many experimented with new religions. There is now solid statistical evidence of the "return" of the older baby boomers to church. David Roozen of Hartford Seminary ran an analysis of the National Opinion Research Center (NORC) data for the years 1982–84 and compared it with the years 1972–74. About one third of the older baby boomers attended church in the early seventies, while in the early eighties 43% attended three or more times per month. Gallup poll data for average church/synagogue attendance of United States adults continues to support this finding.

Roozen found a correlation between political views and church participation. Participation of political liberals declined over the decade, while that of political conservatives increased. However, the study found baby boomers returning to denominations across the theological spectrum, not just to conservative churches. The study also found that parents were more likely to have increased their church attendance, while there was no change in the participation rates for never-married baby boomers.

Warren Hartman, Director of Research for the United Methodist Board of Discipleship, notes that adults aged thirty-five to forty-five are a growing edge for the United Methodist Church and notes three groups within that population. "The first is a sizeable group who are quite conservative, looking for dogmatic interpretations in Scripture ... this group doesn't really identify with a congregation but is likely to identify with a small study group within the congregation. The second group still holds to a social conscience developed in the 1960s and sees the church as an instrument of change ... they may be involved in inner-city projects, homelessness, or teaching underprivileged kids. The third group, less easily defined is 'neo-traditionalist'—conservative but supportive of the congregation—and likely to seek leadership positions within the local church." Hartman also notes the tendency for many in this group to want basic studies in Bible and theology.

Baby boomer values and experiences continue to shape church life in new ways even as this group moves past young adulthood. Churchgoing baby boomers may tend more towards political conservatism now, but many still tend to be "liberal" on "lifestyle issues." Compared with twenty years ago, four times as many of this age group are divorced, and four times as many are living together outside of marriage. As a group, they tend not to disapprove of couples living together outside of marriage. Says baby boomer William McKinney, a sociologist at Hartford Seminary, "That is not to say that the baby boomers are amoral, they just believe that the individual is the final arbiter of what is right and wrong."

The Rev. Robert Jenkins, pastor of a large congregation of baby boomers, notes, "They ask the question 'Why?' a lot and don't just assume that if the church said it it must be true." He attributes a certain caution regarding institutional allegiance to the Vietnam War experience, and notes that while baby boomers attend church with a frequency similar to other generations at their age, they are less likely to be full-fledged members. Gabriel Fackre, professor from Andover, notes that it is something of a surprise that the baby boomers have not established alternative churches or institutions, but still, "They are not settling for the system as it is." Clearly both Jenkins and Fackre are describing the "Challengers."

Money is an issue for baby boomers. Despite media presentations of yuppies, most baby boomers are not doing as well as their parents financially, and higher levels of family income are maintained almost solely by two-wage-earner households. They are as likely to volunteer time as other groups are, but they are less likely to be high givers. According to a Yankelovich study, only 25% of baby boomers give 3% or more of their income to religious or charitable causes. The Rev. Randall Updegraff-Spleth, a pastor to a new congregation of affluent baby boomers, suggests that it is useful to begin stewardship education with baby boomers by talking about how they use discretionary dollars, those not already committed to housing, transportation, child care etc. While not stopping there, he points to studies indicating that peak levels of giving are reached only after seven to ten years in any case.

Randy further reiterates the point that "Boomers are the consummate consumer ... do not expect to generate significant giving if everything about the congregation's program is not geared to quality." He reiterates what several studies and observers have noted; baby-boomers are bringing something of a consumer mentality to their churchgoing. As political analysts are also finding, one cannot count on the old "brand loyalty." Churches welcoming many baby boomers find that at least half come from other denominational backgrounds.

Looking forward, a study of primarily younger baby boomers carried out by the Lutheran Church in America found, "Traditional church concerns for such things as denominational pedigree, rightness of doctrine, or constancy in the practice of piety do not seem to be what will capture the loyalty of baby boomers. ... Baby boomers, as perhaps other age groups, seem to prefer a community of believers that helps them feel wanted and needed, offers a friendly atmosphere, accentuates the positive, at times challenges them physically, spiritually, intellectually, and financially, and includes them in leadership." Or, as Doug Walrath has put it "outsiders are looking for insiders who are able to help them find a meaningful faith."

The Baby Boom Generation. Prepared by the American Council on Life Insurance and the Health Insurance Association of America. 1983. Proprietary Report.

The Baby Boom generation in Congregations of the Lutheran Church in America. Division of Parish Services. Lutheran Church in America. Philadelphia. 1986.

DPS Study of Young Adults: September 4, 1981. Unpublished report of the Department of Parish Services. LCA. Philadelphia. 1981.

Roschen, John Franklin. "Coming, Ready or Not: The Baby-Boom Generation's Challenge to the Church in the Eighties and Nineties. Owatonna, Minnesota—A Case Study." 1984. D.Min. Thesis. United Theological Seminary of the Twin Cities. 3000 Fifth Street Northwest, New Brighton, MN 55112. Copyright by the author. ". . . it is too easy to generalize about the baby-boom generation. . . ."

Updegraff-Spleth, Randall "The Greening of the Church," *Vanguard* April/May/June 1986. Christian Church. Indianapolis.

"Voices of the Future" Project E.D.E.N. report from Presbyterian Men, New York. 1987.

Walrath, Douglas: "Why some people might go back to Church" Review of Religious Research, Sup. 21 #4 :471.

For further reading:
Additions to the Baby Boom Bibliography

Hargrove, Barbara. *The Emerging New Class: Implications for Church and Society,* Pilgrim Press, New York. 1986. An overview of the twenty-two million young baby boomers in the "gray area" between professional and laboring ranks.

Hershey, Terry. *Young Adult Ministry,* Group Books, Loveland, CO. 1986. Good solid step-by-step background and approach for developing a ministry with groups in the eighteen to thirty-five age range.

Kettle, John. *The Big Generation,* McClelland and Stewart, Toronto. 1980. The 1980 imprint does not date the value of this work as background reading on Canada's baby-boom generation, born in the years 1951–66, and thus slightly younger than U.S. baby boomers on the whole.

Lesher, Emerson L., *The Muppie Manual,* Good Books, Intercourse, PA. 1985. Subtitled "The Mennonite Urban Professional's Handbook for Humility and Success," this short book is a delightful and insightful spoof of the lifestyle and language of some of the most dedicated young church members who are "in but not of the world."

Light, Paul C., *Baby Boomers,* W. W. Norton. New York. 1988. Based largely on public opinion surveys, this book's value lies in its inclusiveness. It is not limited to one segment of the baby boom, such as the so-called yuppies.

Parks, Sharon. *The Critical Years,* Harper and Row, San Francisco. 1986. A solid academic work building on academic theory, this work turns a spotlight on the "young adult" period of faith-development between adolescence and "mature adulthood."

Others Not Reviewed

Byerly, Greg, *The Baby Boom: a selective annotated bibliography,* Lexington Books. Lexington, MA 1985.

Phillips, Michael, *What's Really Happening: Baby Boom II Comes of Age,* Clear Glass Publications, Bodega, CA. 1984.

Makower, Joel. *Boom: Talkin' about our Generation* [an anecdotal, illustrated history of 1955–75], Contemporary Books. Chicago. 1985.

Michaels, Joan. *Living Contradictions: The Women of the Baby Boom Come of Age,* Simon and Schuster. New York. 1982.

Urbanska, Wanda. *The Singular Generation: Young Americans in the 1980s,* Doubleday. 1986.

Organization

Center for The New Leadership (The Project on the Vietnam Generation) 1000 Connecticut Ave., NW, Suite 9, Washington, DC 20036.

Additional Notes on References and Research Cited

Data on national church attendance rates comes from the Princeton Religious Research Center, Princeton, New Jersey, which reports religious data from Gallup Polls in annual editions of *Religion in America. The Unchurched American* and *Faith Development and Your Ministry* are available from the same source. Other Gallup Poll figures concerning the relative importance of social values such as family life are reported in *Emerging Trends* published by the Princeton Religious Research Center.

Further data on values of eighteen- to twenty-four-year-olds comes from a transnational study reported in 1982 by the Centre for Applied Research on the Apostolate in Washington, D.C.

Data on childrearing goals come from a 1924 study replicated in 1978 and reported by Duane Alwin of the Institute for Social Research at the University of Michigan.

Reanalysis of "baby boom" participation rates between the 1970s and 1980s was conducted by Dr. David Roozen of Hartford Seminary, Hartford, Connecticut.

The comment of John Pollock concerning the strength of the "religious factor" in American life was quoted in *The Washington Post* (April 3, 1981, page C14) on the release of *The Connecticut Mutual Life Report on American Values in the Eighties: The Impact of Belief,* from the Connecticut Mutual Life Insurance Company, 140 Garden Street, Hartford, Connecticut.

"Transadulthood: New Thoughts on Older Youth" by Robert Ross appeared in PACE 6 (February 1975), published by St. Mary's College Press, Winona, Minnesota.

Medical perspectives on early adulthood were reviewed in *Daedalus,* Spring 1976.

"The Religious Dimension of Life During Adolescence" by J. Anne Devitt Trevelyan is a Ph.D. dissertation at Harvard University, 1978.

The Dayton Young Adult Ministry Study, regarded as a barometer for the nation, was first conducted in 1976 and reported as "Attitudes, Values, and Lifestyles of Young Adults in Greater Dayton" by the Miami Valley Young Adult Ministry, Fairborn, Ohio.

In addition to published summaries, the Religious Education Association released raw data from the project "Faith Development in the Adult Life Cycle" in conjunction with conferences in 1987.

The term "belief without belonging" is generally credited to Carl Dudley, author of *Where Have All Our People Gone?* (Pilgrim Press, 1979).

The remark quoted from Myron B. Bloy, Jr. is from "A Report:

Parish Ministry to Higher Education in the Episcopal Church" published by the National Institute for Campus Ministry. Bloy made
many contributions to work with students, but unfortunately both
he and the Institute he headed are now deceased.

The Rev. James R. Adams is Rector of St. Mark's Episcopal
Church in Washington. His most recent book is *So You Think
You're Not Religious* (Cowley Publications, 1989).

Alban Institute Research

Interviews regarding young adult ministry were begun with twenty-
eight local church pastors in Montgomery County, Maryland in the
early 1970s with assistance from a grant from the Episcopal Church.
In 1976, this work was brought under the auspices of The Alban Institute and expanded with a grant from the Lilly Endowment. Insights and techniques were refined in working with various judica-
tories and congregations in the Washington, D.C. area. Additional
explorations were conducted with various congregations, campus
ministry units and U.S. Army chaplains. Under the auspices of the
United Ministries in Education *Students, Churches, and Higher Education* was published by Judson Press. *Religious Development of
Young Adults: Implications for Young Soldiers* was published by the
U.S. Army Chaplain Board.

Further research on congregational youth ministry was explored
with ten selected congregations in the U.S. and Panama. That research was published by the Episcopal Church under the title *Let's
Put Young People in Their Place.*

In 1981, the Lilly Endowment funded through The Alban Institute the 30+ Ministry Project. It was so named because it was designed initially to test the assumption held by many pastors that
younger people who drop out of the church will come back when
they are past age thirty. We were aware of the fact that the number
of persons in their thirties would be increasing in this decade due
to the aging of the baby boom generation. In the early stages of the
project it became apparent that the average age of persons returning to active congregational participation was lower than thirty.
Therefore the population sampled was broadened to include ages
twenty-five to forty. Other early findings and hypotheses gained
from a review of the literature were published in an Alban Institute
monograph, *30 Year-Olds and the Church: Ministry With the Baby
Boom Generation.*

Interviews were conducted in twenty-five congregations of various denominations around the United States. All sampled congregations participated voluntarily, most having been initially nominated

by officials in their denomination. From 142 congregations volunteering and supplying preliminary information, the final twenty-five were selected to give a sample roughly reflecting the United States in terms of geographic region, location (urban, suburban, rural), ethnic composition, socio-economic level, size of church membership, and denomination. Based on the information gathered from the respondents it appears that Christians having a literalist interpretation of the Bible are underrepresented in this study as are the very poor. Due to the small sample size and the loss of some congregations after initial selection, some important groups whose experience may be significantly different are not included. Among these losses we note that no Spanish speaking, Greek Orthodox, or Native American churches were included in the final sample. Because the sample congregations volunteered, there is a bias towards congregations open to outside investigation. Among other things this is a bias towards people who have some degree of comfort with social science investigation of religion. Overall, we expect that this study is most representative of, and will be most useful to, congregations that are middle-class and theologically "middle of the road."

In each congregation interviews were conducted with the pastor, assistant pastor (if any), other staff, lay leaders, and with a group of people in the twenty-five to forty-year-old age range. These interviews were directed toward gaining a view of the congregation's overall ministry, its particular ministry to this age group, and the way in which the ministry was perceived by the people in this age group. Additional life-story information was gathered from the twenty-five to forty-year-olds concerning their participation in the church since age eighteen and the manner in which they had come to be a part of this congregation. There are a total of 282 individual returns in this set. As participants in these groups were persons who voluntarily came out to a meeting at a church on a weekday evening, we suspect that they may be more favorably disposed to the church and more active than other churchgoers in the age range.

Individual life-story interviews of an hour-and-a-half in length were conducted with three or four persons in each location. One hundred and two of these individual interviews were conducted in the course of the project. (Returns from three test congregations were excluded from final tallies, leaving ninety-three individual returns from twenty-five congregations in this data set). Those interviewed were volunteers, invited to participate by a pastor or lay coordinator. Questions in these interviews focused primarily on the individual's relationship with religious organizations and religious practice from early childhood until the present. The decision to focus on the "religious journey" rather than on the more inclusive concept of "spiritual pilgrimage" or "faith development" was made due to the particular aims and limitation of this study. We note that for Jean Haldane's study, *Religious Pilgrimage* (Alban Institute, 1975), in which the personal religious journey is differentiated from the process of religious socialization, four interviews over the course of several months were required. A longer interview format more focused on the spiritual journey might uncover a greater incidence of personal religious experience and faith statements as a basis for life action than reported here. Written questionnaires as well as verbal responses were collected from all who participated in the group or individual interviews. The interviews in this study were conducted between September 1981 and August 1982 by Robert Gribbon and Cecilia Braveboy of The Alban Institute.

The ongoing investigations and results of these Alban Institute studies were previously published in a series of separate monographs as follows: *The Problem of Faith-Development in Young Adults; Congregations, Students, and Young Adults; 30-Year-Olds and the Church: Ministry with the Baby Boom Generation; When People Seek the Church;* and *Half the Congregation: Ministry with Eighteen to Forty-Year-Olds*

Burkhart, Roy. *Understanding Youth*. New York: Abingdon Press, 1938.

Cox, Norman Wade. *Youth's Return to Faith*. Philadelphia: Judson Press, 1938.

Donne, John S. *A Search for God in Time and Memory*. New York: Macmillan Publishing Co., 1967.

Erikson, Erik. *Childhood and Society*. 2d ed. New York: W W Norton & Co., 1950.

———. *Identity: Youth and Crisis*. New York: W W Norton & Co., 1968.

———. *Young Man Luther*. New York: W W Norton & Co., 1958.

Fowler, James. *Becoming Adult, Becoming Christian*. San Francisco: Harper & Row, 1984.

——— and Sam Keen. *Life Maps*. Waco, TX: Word Books, 1978.

———. *Stages of Faith*. San Francisco: Harper & Row, 1981.

Gilligan, Carol. *In a Different Voice: Psychological Theory and Women's Development*. Cambridge: Harvard University Press, 1982.

Glasser, William. *The Identity Society*. New York: Harper & Row, 1972, 1975.

Gould, Roger. *Transformations*. New York: Simon & Schuster, 1978.

Haldane, Jean M. *Religious Pilgrimage*. Washington: The Alban Institute, Inc., 1975.

Hale, J. Russell. *The Unchurched: Who They Are and Why They Stay Away*. San Francisco: Harper & Row, 1980.

Havinghurst, R. J. *Human Development and Education*. New York: Longmans Green & Co., 1953.

Hershey, Terry. *Young Adult Ministry*. Loveland, CO: Group Books, 1986.

Hoge, Dean. *Converts, Dropouts, and Returnees.* New York: Pilgrim Press, 1981.

———— and Roozen, ed. *The Unchurched American: A Second Look.* Hartford: Hartford Seminary Foundation, 1980.

Jung, Carl G. *Modern Man in Search of a Soul.* New York: Harcourt Brace Jovanovich, Inc., 1933.

Kegan, Robert. *The Evolving Self.* Cambridge: Harvard University Press, 1982.

Kohlberg, Lawrence. *The Philosophy of Moral Development.* San Francisco: Harper & Row, 1981.

Levinson, Daniel. *Seasons of a Man's Life.* New York: Alfred A. Knopf, 1978.

Loevinger, Jane. *Ego Development.* San Francisco: Jossey-Bass, Inc. Publishers, 1977.

Lorimier, Jacques, Roger Graveline, and April Aubert. *Identity and Faith in Young Adults.* New York: Paulist Press, 1973.

Mowry, Charles E. *The Church and the New Generation.* Nashville: Abingdon Press, 1969.

Parks, Sharon. *The Critical Years.* San Francisco: Harper & Row, 1986.

Perry, William G., Jr. *Forms of Intellectual and Ethical Development in the College Years.* New York: Holt, Rinehart & Winston, Inc., 1968.

Reed, Bruce D. *The Dynamics of Religion; Process & Movement in Christian Churches.* London: Darton, Longman & Todd, 1978.

————. *The Task of the Church and the Role of its Members.* Washington: The Alban Institute, Inc., 1975.

Savage, John S. *The Bored and Apathetic Church Member.* Pittsford, NY: LEAD Consultants.

Sheehy, Gail. *Passages.* New York: E. P. Dutton, 1976.

Stokes, Kenneth. *Faith Is a Verb.* Mystic, CT: Twenty-third Publications, 1989.

Strommen, Brekke and Johnson Underwager. *A Study of Generations.* Minneapolis: Augsburg, 1972.

Tracy, Fredrick. *The Psychology of Adolescence.* New York: Macmillan Publishing Co., 1925.

Vaillant, George E. *Adaptation to Life.* Boston: Little, Brown, & Co., 1977.

Walrath, Douglas. *Frameworks: Patterns for Living and Believing Today.* New York: Pilgrim Press, 1987.

Westerhoff, John H., III. *Will Our Children Have Faith?* New York: Seabury Press, 1976

The Alban Institute:
an invitation to membership

The Alban Institute, begun in 1979, believes that the congregation is essential to the task of equipping the people of God to minister in the church and the world. A multi-denominational membership organization, the Institute provides on-site training, educational programs, consulting, research, and publishing for hundreds of churches across the country.

The Alban Institute invites you to be a member of this partnership of laity, clergy, and executives—a partnership that brings together people who are raising important questions about congregational life and people who are trying new solutions, making new discoveries, finding a new way of getting clear about the task of ministry. The Institute exists to provide you with the kinds of information and resources you need to support your ministries.

Join us now and enjoy these benefits:

CONGREGATIONS, The Alban Journal, a highly respected journal published six times a year, to keep you up to date on current issues and trends.

Inside Information, Alban's quarterly newsletter, keeps you informed about research and other happenings around Alban. Available to members only.

Publications Discounts:

☐ 15% for Individual, Retired Clergy, and Seminarian Members
☐ 25% for Congregational Members
☐ 40% for Judicatory and Seminary Executive Members

Discounts on Training and Education Events

Write our Membership Department at the address below or call us at (202) 244-7320 for more information about how to join The Alban Institute's growing membership, particularly about Congregational Membership in which 12 designated persons receive all benefits of membership.

The Alban Institute, Inc.
4125 Nebraska Avenue, NW
Washington, DC 20016